the
secret
lives
of
boys

the
secret
lives
of
boys

inside the
raw emotional
world of
male teens

Malina Saval

BASIC
BOOKS

New York

Copyright © 2009 by Malina Sarah Saval Mindell

Published by Basic Books,
A Member of the Perseus Books Group
387 Park Avenue South
New York, NY 10016

Designed by Pauline Brown
Text set in 11.75-point Stemple Garamond

Library of Congress Cataloging-in-Publication Data
Saval, Malina.
 The secret lives of boys : inside the raw emotional world of male teens
/ Malina Saval.
     p. cm.
 Includes bibliographical references and index.
 ISBN 978-0-465-00254-2 (alk. paper)
 1. Teenage boys—United States—Psychology. 2. Emotions in adolescence. I. Title.

 HQ797.S28 2009
 155.5'320973—dc22

                                        2008049703

10 9 8 7 6 5 4 3 2 1

For Boaz, the best little boy
in the whole wide world

Tom was a glittering hero once more.
There were some that believed
he would be President yet . . .

—MARK TWAIN,
The Adventures of Tom Sawyer

Contents

the
secret
lives
of
boys

introduction
Madolescence

Mad•o•les•cence *n.* **1.** Adolescence in males **2.** The messy, inscrutable period between puberty and adulthood often misunderstood and misinterpreted by the adult population[1]

One of those things that has always bothered me is that people think boys aren't emotional. You've never been around boys if you don't think they're emotional. They're highly emotional.
—*Ritch C. Savin-Williams, professor and chair of human development at Cornell University*

There is a general consensus that American culture has failed our boys, and *they* have failed *us.* We hear that they are falling behind in grammar school, in high school, in college. In numerous articles and books they are portrayed as being limp-as-spaghetti, verbally challenged creatures lacking the emotional resolve or innate intellectual wherewithal to react and respond to society's demands on them. They are repressed, they are troubled and sad, society has somehow sucked away boys' ability to emote (glaring examples of this attitude rest in such annals as William Pollack's *Real Boys: Rescuing Our Sons from the Myths of Boyhood;* and *Raising Cain: Protecting the Emotional Life of Boys,* by psychologists Dan Kindlon and Michael Thompson). So now we're instructed that we must *teach* them how to be emotional before it's too late. It's not just that boys *don't* cry, we are now told—it's that they don't know *how*.

My goal, as I set out to write this book, was to find a well-balanced cross-section of teenage boys from all walks of life—rich, poor, white, black, Jewish, Christian, Muslim, agnostic—so that each parent opening this book could find his or her son on one of its pages. In the end, each boy's personality, and not his race, religion, or socioeconomic condition, was what prevailed during my interviews as the most crucial and telling characteristic. I chose to focus on a handful of boys who seemed the most enthusiastic in telling their stories. Ultimately, it wasn't about what his last name was or whether he attended church or synagogue or mosque or whether he lived in the country or in the city that made each of these boys relatable. Because boys, like all of us, are far more alike than different.

Despite a rash over the past ten years of junior chick lit manifestos penned by career women in multiple fields on everything from anorexia to rape to promiscuity to depression to shopping, there's little to match it from the guy's perspective. Girls get most of the press. The scant material on teenage males tends to focus on the white upper middle class; books on minority male teens often reduce them to thug-like stereotypes. Such groundbreaking books as *Reviving Ophelia* and *Queen Bees and Wannabes* present young women as multidimensional figures with a range of personal characteristics. These seminal works paved the way for a veritable glut of girl power books focusing on issues of female self-worth, fostering autonomy and strategies on how young women coming from every social group and possessing a range of talents can succeed in high school, college, and the workforce.

Yet most available books about boys, the odd cover story in *Newsweek*, and featured segments on *20/20* focus on our young men as a homogeneous whole, a collective entity with no discernibly varying characteristics. Boys are often thought of as unknowable enigmas who *all* seem to need help. Boys are in crisis. Boys have ADD. Boys are unemotional. Boys don't talk. Boys are on the verge of apocalyptic self-destruction. Over the course of the past decade, boys have been reduced to an anxiety-inducing headline.

Having tracked the lives of boys over the past several years as both an educator and a journalist writing articles about teens, I've found that many of our views of boys are nowhere close to reality. Boys cry. Boys emote. Some don't, of course, but some girls don't either. Some boys talk *more* than girls. Many of the boys I spoke with gabbed nonstop for hours.

As a teacher, I have a perspective on boys that most parents don't attain. For the most part, in the classes I have taught at the high school, junior high, and elementary levels, boys have always been among the most articulate, thoughtful, and enthusiastic students.

Boys, if they *are* in crisis, are in as much a state of crisis as the rest of us.

Clinicians and researchers have provided valuable learning tools that help us understand adolescent behavior. Many scholars have established theories and arguments about boys' fledgling standardized scores, plunging grades, rates of depression, and use of drugs. There are some figures that understandably spur alarm—such as the spike in boys' suicide rates—which in turn raise the right kind of awareness.

But not every statistic that's shared with us foretells gloom and doom. In fact, social science data today points to a more hopeful outlook about boys than it has in decades past. Declining rates of illicit drug use and juvenile crime (the rate of juvenile males in prison is *half* of its historic 1993 high), rising SAT scores, and increasing graduation rates have been reported by the National Center for Education Statistics and the U.S. Department of Justice. Boys in fourth, eighth, and twelfth grades are scoring slightly higher on math tests than they did in the 1990s.[2] The headline of an uplifting *Time* cover story reads, "The Myth About Boys: Experts Say Boys Are in Trouble. Here's Why They've Got It Wrong."

Nonetheless, these statistics don't necessarily reflect the core truth about teenage boys in regard to their personalities and private lives, and they don't always tell the whole story. The more time I spent with boys, the more I wondered, What if we got to know boys through a methodology that examined elements outside of test scores, grades, and numerical figures?

Beyond the studies—the bar graphs, pie charts, and percentages—I wondered what it would be like to experience life with teenage boys on their own home turf, to crouch down in the proverbial foxhole with them as they study for tests, watch their favorite movies, woo girlfriends, face rejection, fill their prescriptions, shop for clothes, do or choose *not* to do their homework.

As I started researching this book, I began an eye-opening, patience-flexing, awe-inspiring, and sometimes disconcerting journey into the inner sanctum of American boyhood culture. I interviewed people who work in high school education, contacted graduate school professors, and cold-called student and youth religious organizations in cities and states across the nation. I contacted the parents of former students. I talked to the younger siblings of colleagues and friends. I sought out boys through every outlet that would allow me to spend time with them not confined to a classroom or clinical setting.

My mission was to secure a small group of boys and focus on each one over a period of months. I selected the ten boys you will meet in this book on the basis of their insight and their courage to speak candidly about topics ranging from depression to sex to drugs to parental resentment. In getting to know these boys, I drafted an initial list of interview questions. I asked many of the boys the same questions, which changed as our conversations changed, as did the scope of the questions. I wound up spending anywhere from four months to two years observing, interviewing, and chatting with the boys as they went about everyday life.

Parents were intrigued by the idea of their sons participating in this book, but they also expressed numerous concerns. They wanted to make sure that their words and ideas were not taken out of context. One parent feared that I would have this "preconceived notion of who his son was" and then try to mold his child into that boxed description or category. Many parents were eager to make sure that I did not have a slanted agenda. The concept that a journalist wanted to study boys, to hang out with them, to see what makes them tick, was worrisome to many parents and guardians. However, most parents agreed with their boys in their decision to participate. They did so, they told me, because they were excited about the idea that the book would shed light on twenty-first-century teen culture.

Boys today face situations and problems that are vastly different from issues earlier generations have faced. Teenage boys twenty years ago didn't have to worry about cyber sex or cyber bullies. They didn't have to deal with international terrorism. They didn't have to deal with other kids slamming their reputation on Facebook. The constant stimulation of mass media and in-your-face popular culture means that boys have to adapt to a veritable maelstrom of influences—some good, others detrimental—and learn new ways of dealing with the overwhelming opportunities available to them in the way of sex, drugs, and mental stimulation.

There are countless media outlets through which teens can openly (and often anonymously) communicate with the world, unknown to their parents. Courtesy of the Internet, society has become one big emotional free-for-all, a culture where everybody blogs about what mood they're in from one moment to the next, no matter how intimate or dirty the details. This can weigh heavily on a teen who may not be ready to handle it.

A recent article in *Scientific American Mind* reveals that changes in the prefrontal cortex (the region of the brain that controls decision making and voluntary behavior) may still be "pruning," or developing, well into our twenties. In other words, boys who are still neurologically immature and possess imperfect behavior control are subjected to some pretty dizzying stimuli. That teenagers in general are doing as well as they are in the face of all this is worth applauding.

Despite the various media outlets available to teens to air their feelings, many of the boys I spoke with felt steeped in loneliness. When the boys expressed how lonely they felt at times, it was because they didn't believe there was anybody out there who understood them. They felt "different" from everyone else and lacked soul mate figures with whom they could share their innermost thoughts. They didn't always feel like they had close friends to talk to, and their parents, they told me, didn't always want to know the truth—about their children or about themselves. They weren't intentionally elusive when it came to what they told their parents; rather, their parents just weren't ready to hear what they had to say. I wished that the boys I spoke with could meet one another and discover for themselves that despite how different they all thought they were, they actually had a great deal in common in terms of their feelings and the aching desire to connect to other people.

The boys told me straight out that they were not just looking for someone to talk *to*, but someone to talk *with*. They want you to hear what they have to say, and they are inviting responsive conversation. As one mother of a teenage boy I spoke with put it after reading a draft of her child's chapter, "I feel like I just met my kid."

While I was working on this book, my understanding of boys came under challenge and evolved along the way. Heading into my research, I admittedly clung to some of my own beliefs about certain types of boys. I was surprised to discover that the teenage dad I spoke with was not only involved in his child's upbringing but had much in common in terms of parenting style with many fathers I know in their thirties and forties. As a mom, I was shocked to discover that this teen and I had much to talk about in the way of diapers, sippy cups, and chicken pox vaccinations.

Fashion, I discovered, is a way teenage boys express their personality and emerging sense of identity, change the way they feel about themselves, and sometimes change the way others feel about *them*. The boys dressed to mark themselves as individuals and reinforce a sense of self and originality. Sure, most boys didn't sit around flipping through *Teen Vogue*, but I met plenty of boys who wanted to look like the Patrick Dempsey fashion pictorial in *Details*. I met boys who opted for such shopping outposts as Abercrombie & Fitch, with techno music thumping though the store and a steady procession of swingy, ponytailed girls in T-shirts, shrunken sweaters, and napkin-size miniskirts embossed with little AF logos be-bopping their way toward the dressing room.

I discovered that boys, despite their individual problems, flaws, and proverbial crosses to bear—or perhaps because of all these things—are working in very brave ways to create lives for themselves that are notably and distinctively different and infinitely more inspiring than some insipidly collective globule.

Teenage boys today are not bound by any one set of rules or regulations. They are not all stymied by social expectations. Of course, this is not to say that we don't still make unreasonable demands of grown (and growing) men. But boys today are working to defy such expectations. They are waiting longer to have sex. They are pursuing careers based not primarily on socioeconomic prospects but on passion. They are taking dance lessons. They're wearing pink. They're crying in front of their girlfriends and *not* feeling emasculated. They're crying—*period*.

Teenage male cliques and labels have come a long way since the staid 1980s when *Breakfast Club* categories of brains, druggies, and jocks were based solely on similar social standing. Today's "madolescent" youth culture is multifaceted and complicated, its social map ever expanding. For better or worse, the pecking order is less predictable. There are far more subcategories, some damning and negative, others further accentuating the propitious aspects of individuation. No longer are drugs, sex, and SAT scores the sole criteria for delineating droves of boys; you can be both captain of the football team and class valedictorian. It's nothing to be a pot-smoking Stanford-bound burnout enrolled in a Kaplan course. With 6.7 percent of youth between the ages of twelve and seventeen smoking marijuana—making it the most commonly used illicit substance among teens—many kids don't even consider it a drug.[3]

Whereas in past generations, boys were branded mostly according to class and culture, choosing associates on the basis of necessity because nobody else wanted to be friends with them, adolescent males in such diverse places as Los Angeles, Boston, and Omaha now can choose among a cornucopia of social groups. Boys informed me that there are also many subcategories of social groups in which they can belong.

Boys today are responding to the world around them in ways that reflect the cultural context in which they live. In this book I describe how one boy combats obsessive-compulsive disorder, how another deals with his homosexuality, how yet another deals with being bullied in school. I profile how each boy deals with his concerns and joys and frustrations in a way that makes sense to him. These boys projected loneliness, confusion, resilience, and fear. As well as joy and hope. These boys expressed hope as they discussed future career prospects, artistic interests, college, girls. Boys were romantic. Boys were sensitive. They cared about their parents, their siblings, their friends. One boy told me that he noticed how hypocritical girls could be, how they turned their backs on one another so quickly and yet spoke all the time of "what good friends" they were. Boys, he asserted, didn't need to say anything in this regard. Theirs was more of a tacit understanding between them, an unspoken loyalty. And that, he said, made their friendships stronger.

In my interviews with leading specialists in the field, I learned that when it comes to male friendships, some studies point to boys being more sensitive than girls. Boys, these studies conclude, are more hard-pressed to forgive and move on when they've felt a sense of betrayal. Their pain cut much deeper. They may not sob publicly, but that may not mean that they've shut down emotionally. Quite the contrary—I found that the boys I spoke with were emotional sieves.

Niobe Way, professor of applied psychology at New York University's Steinhardt School of Culture, Education, and Human Development and the coauthor of *Adolescent*

Boys: Exploring Diverse Cultures of Boyhood, concurs: "There's a whole notion of whether or not boys actually are, in some ways, more vulnerable than girls." Way's landmark research has focused on the friendships and the emotional development of adolescent boys in such far-ranging places as Nanjing, China, and New York City. "In one finding, boys who had been betrayed in their friendships were not willing to forgive and forget," Way told me. "They were much more resistant to doing that than girls. The flexibility is just not there."[4]

Loyalty, posits Way, is one of the most undersold qualities of boys. When a boy feels that a friend has turned his back on him, that betrayal is searing, and the damage can be irreversible. Unfortunately this rigidity in boys is often misunderstood as lack of emotion.

Teens also tend to lead secret lives. A developmental shift occurs as they mature from adolescence to adulthood. Suddenly details that teens might have divulged to their parents years ago become information hoarded or kept between themselves and their peers. James Garbarino, chair in humanistic psychology at Loyola University Chicago and coauthor with Claire Bedard of *Parents Under Siege: Why You Are the Solution, Not the Problem in Your Child's Life,* offers a humbling view on adolescent secrecy: sometimes there's nothing we can do about it.

Garbarino and Bedard affirm that, at a certain level, no matter how we try to be the friend or try not to look like we're trying, a teenager's natural impulse is to construct his own secret world. Developing new connections, discovering new relationships, and forging new interests are a source of strength, of bolstering clout and self-confidence. As Garbarino and Bedard note, "When we get into our teens, we learn that information is power. To successfully conceal information makes us feel powerful."[5]

In their research, Garbarino and Bedard polled a group of 275 first-year undergraduates at Cornell University and asked them to describe the "worst thing, in the sense of most dangerous or troubling" that they had been involved with as high school students and that their parents *did not know* about. An astounding one-quarter of the surveyed students said they had considered suicide, and 87 percent of those students' parents never knew. Eleven percent had sampled hard drugs such as cocaine and Ecstasy, and 92 percent of their parents never knew. Twenty-three percent admitted to driving under the influence of alcohol, and 94 percent of their parents never knew. Garbarino and Bedard conclude that much of the time, parents are not to blame for what they don't know about their kids. Sometimes, they assert, the issue is not what parents are asking their teenagers, but what information teens choose to share with their parents.[6]

Consistent with Garbarino and Bedard's findings, sometimes the boys I interviewed chose to omit certain details of their lives based on pride or fear or even what their mood was on the day that we spoke. On rare occasions they would relay creative versions of the truth, the way they *wished* events had transpired. I discovered such omissions and imaginative retellings when, days following such interviews, boys would contact me with the real story. Indeed, shifting values and ideals are an intrinsic part of boyhood, as well as one of its most propitious and liberating attributes. During interviews a teen would make a sweeping statement and then, in a follow-up meeting, assiduously recant. These impromptu outbursts provided moments of catharsis, of emotional exploration. One boy spent two hours over sandwiches and fries vehemently bashing his working-class parents for their ignorance when it came to college applications. A week later we met up again and he admitted that maybe his reaction was a little severe. Mood swings, developments on the school front, evolving family dynamics, even hormones—all of these factors accounted for changes of heart.

Ultimately this book can only be one version of the truth about boys today in America.

The teenage boys I spoke with chose to share some of their most intimate secrets with me. Part of this had to do with the fact that I wasn't their parent. I wasn't going to ground them or, even worse, exhibit an unctuous display of approval that might embarrass them in front of their friends. They knew that what they talked about would make its way into print and that eventually their parents would read it, but being one step removed created a comfortable buffer zone for these boys. For many of the boys, sharing raw personal details for the first time in their lives was emotionally liberating.

While some parents were thrilled to discover their son's secret life because it gave them a more intimate understanding of him as an individual, others feared that I was going to find out that their boys were ticking time bombs. I spoke with several parents who wondered how I planned to weave a discussion of boys and guns throughout the book, referencing such dismal incidents as Columbine, Virginia Tech, and a 2008 shooting at a junior high school in Oxnard, California, that left a fifteen-year-old brain dead. Unfortunately, many in our culture believe that there is an entire subset of boys building bombs and cooking up Molotov cocktails in their basements while plotting the destruction of the world. Throughout my conversations with parents, I maintained that while the Columbine tragedy and atrocities at other schools represent dark days in our history, it is problematic to connect such acts of violence to most teenage boys in the United States today. While writing this book, I encountered numerous examples of boys rallying to create a sense of peace and justice in their home communities. I met boys involved with animal rights groups and antiviolence organizations. I met boys who helped create social programming for at-risk youth. I met boys who were involved in theater companies that raised awareness about GLBT issues.

Is adolescent boyhood culture really as grim as the now infamous Larry Clark film *Kids*, about a promiscuous teenage boy in New York City who unknowingly infects his young virginal conquests with HIV? Is it as nihilistic as Nick Cassavetes's *Alpha Dog*, an edgy indie flick tracking the lives of amoral underworld drug lords in the 1990s? Or was it, on the flip side, as frothy and mindless as the stoner comedy *Harold & Kumar Go to White Castle* and its sequel *Harold & Kumar Escape from Guantanamo Bay*?

I have discovered again and again that some of boys' best-kept secrets are *good* ones that they are eager to share. These boys remain refreshingly propitious about the future, spinning pragmatic and often chronically optimistic versions of their adult life to come. They may not all wind up living behind a white picket fence, but they're not all going to San Quentin either.

Some of what the boys said may offend others, may seem raw and unsettling, but for the sake of authenticity I have maintained their voices throughout. This book is truly a product of the boys themselves. Their words fill every page.

To that end, the boys supplied the titles for their own chapters. These titles also reflect archetypes or genres of adolescent male youth. Some are self-reflective ("Indie Fuck"), whereas others reflect how they feel society views *them*. "The Rich Kid" believes that's how many people see him—dollar signs trailing his last name like graduate degree credentials. But what people don't see, fears this boy, are the struggles buried beneath the bank account. "The Mini-Adult" is a kid who in former times might have been branded simply a "nerd" without anybody really getting to know him. In coining their own terms, these boys are making it clear that *they, not we,* get to decide who they are.

Indeed, there were other boys that I met, each of them equally fascinating. There was a boy with HIV and a boy who was a preoperative transsexual. There was an evangelical Christian boy active in a youth ministry that crusades against what it calls "the corrupting influence of popular culture." There was a boy who sat in the school library and wept over the brother who took a bullet in the chest and died in his arms. There was a boy whose mother had passed away and whose father didn't know that he was gay. There was a boy whose parents thought that he was gay because he was a virgin. There was a straight boy who was a gay rights activist.

I wanted to write about all of them. But I also wanted to engage boys in such a way that they could open up and explore their feelings and lives in depth, without having to limit any of them (relatively speaking) in terms of time and chapter space. Some of the boys I met initially during the first round of interviews weren't ready to reveal their personal lives in print. Some of the parents weren't ready for their sons to be examined in these pages. Some of the boys simply disappeared on me. Sometimes, I quickly learned, the only earthly creature cooler and more elusive than a young, hot Hollywood celebrity is a teenage boy in the throes of adolescence.

The reward came with the boys who participated in this book. They proved that they are not *all* in crisis. They are not *all* perfect. They are not *all* self-destructive. Teenage boys are *human*. Teenage boys flail, they stumble, they fail, and they succeed. They are brazen and unpredictable. They do not deserve to be hampered or hindered by stereotypes.

Teenage boys have much to teach us all.

The
Indie Fuck

Sometimes, when I get too frustrated with everything, and I need some kind
of release, some way to lessen the pressure and let the steam out my ears, I've
discovered that perfect outlets are my little navy blue pillows. I rush to my room
and bury my face in one and scream into it until I'm hoarse and it feels like my
lungs must have given way, until I feel as if the very capillaries they're made up
of will just burst and I'll drown internally on my own life; I sit up, I pummel
them until my arms ache. And then I scream some more … and when I come
to school all I see is concrete. A concrete jungle full of ugly monstrosities—
they're called my peers. But I'm just another one of them.

—Apollo Lev

I first met Apollo Lev a few years ago when he
slouched through the door of my fourth grade Hebrew
school class. He was my fifteen-year-old teaching assistant,
and I was a part-time teacher logging time between pop cultural journalism assignments and screenwriting gigs, quickly
discovering that working with nine- and ten-year-olds was
surprising, demanding, and inspiring.

Every Wednesday at around 4:15 in the afternoon,
Apollo would reluctantly tumble into class, hooded sweatshirt and jeans frayed within an inch of their existence.
His soft brown hair fell in diagonal wisps across his forehead, his ratty Chuck Taylors one wear away from split-
ting apart at the soles. Some days, Apollo recalled Kieran
Culkin's disgruntled, angst-ridden rebel in the indie cult
classic *Igby Goes Down*, a red and yellow Harry Potter
scarf wagging behind him for emphasis, uttering icy insights
on such matters as American consumerism and supporters

of the fashionable green movement, the new upper-middle-class cause du jour: "People who drive Priuses are people who are from, like, Vermont or New Hampshire and campaigning for more warning stickers on cigarette cartons."

Other times, there was something sunny lurking beneath the thrift store styles. The class clown might crack a comment, and Apollo would cock a lopsided grin. He could be provocative, telling politically incorrect jokes. When a gaggle of buttery-blonde girls bounced into class wearing matching pink tutus and plastic rhinestone tiaras, Apollo's nasal chortle reverberated around the room.

Aside from the disheveled duds, Apollo was the physical embodiment of healthy, rosebud youth. Noting his cherubic features—bright, clear skin, plump lips, a faint smudge of pale cherry pink on each cheek—I never guessed that Apollo was a recovering drug addict who spent much of his early teens scoring speed in the alleyways of Hollywood's boutique-laden Melrose Avenue.

Like so many other young drug addicts, Apollo began his love affair with meth with that One. First. Time. As playwright Arthur Miller once wrote, "Where choice begins, Paradise ends, innocence ends."

Choice is beginning a lot earlier these days and, when it comes to methamphetamine, many kids have ample access. They call it meth, crank, ice, crystal, speed, biker's coffee, poor man's coke, chalk. It's easy to make, burn, inject, and inhale. While the use of meth among teens in grades eight, ten, and twelve has been gradually declining since 1999,[1] per a 2005 Monitoring the Future report, 4.5 percent of high school seniors have tried the highly addictive drug at least once.[2]

As we now know, kids can be creative when it comes to getting a quick fix of speed. They use pseudoephedrine, an ingredient found in cold remedies, to cook meth in makeshift labs. Kids crush Ritalin tabs and snort the powder through a straw, the scratchy rush akin to a cocaine high. According to the National Institute of Mental Health, approximately 2.4 million children between the ages of eight and fifteen in the United States meet the diagnostic criteria for attention deficit hyperactivity disorder (ADHD) and are being treated with such amphetamine-dextroamphetamine and methylphenidate-based stimulants as Adderall, Ritalin, and Dexedrine.[3] Consequently the materials used to make meth are fairly easy to get these days. Many well-intentioned parents race about filling these prescriptions, oblivious to the fact that they are supplying their children and their friends with a drug that can be manipulated and abused.

According to a 2006 Drug Abuse Warning Network report, 48 percent of the estimated 7,873 emergency room visits involving ADHD stimulant medications related to nonmedical use of the drugs, and the rates of these visits were higher for patients twelve through seventeen than they were for patients eighteen and older. In addition, between 1994 and 2004, the number of twelve- to seventeen-year-olds admitted to treatment for meth addiction more than doubled.[4]

While these facts and figures reveal much in the way of how our teens do drugs, they say almost nothing about why teens feel compelled to use them in the first place.

Apollo was fourteen years old when he spent ninety-four days in a tony youth rehab center in California that he dutifully refuses to name. He made friends there, he explains—heroin junkies, pill poppers, pot fiends—whose privacy he needs to respect. As part of his rehabilitation effort Apollo got an after-school job as my teaching assistant. Granted, Apollo never really *assisted*. You could tell by the shallow look in his eyes how unbearably bored he felt in what he obviously perceived as an unstimulating classroom environment. As he once explained to me, to a kid once hooked, life *sans* speed can move pretty damn slow.

Apollo spent most of his time in class straddling a chair at the back of the room reading Tolkien, sci-fi classics, Chuck Palahniuk, and Haruki Murakami novels, and sneaking behind my back when I was busy helping a student to log on to his MySpace account on the spare desktop computer. That year, seemingly every teenage boy wearing a black T-shirt and bangs in his face had his hands on Chuck Palahniuk's *Fight Club*, so I asked Apollo one day why he thought kids like him were so obsessed with the author. "In terms of Palahniuk I know just as many females who read him as I do males," he corrected, "and I find that both sexes who do are in similarly dire need of an expansion of literary taste." Violence in literature could be a girl's thing too, and Apollo, a staunch individualist, was growing tired of how trendy Palahniuk's darkly humorous books had become.

The epic *Fellowship of the Ring* film was also popular that year with teens (who anxiously awaited its much talked about sequel), and Apollo explained why the movie held such mass appeal for boys like him. "Personally, I'm just a fan of all things otherworldly," Apollo told me, shedding light on the sci-fi/fantasy interest shared by many teens. "I find worlds of the imagination to be much more provocative than the one we live in, which, unfortunately, often tends to pale in comparison. About Tolkien, if you can't enjoy it, then you're just shortsighted."

I'd try to encourage Apollo to become more involved in classroom activity, but he was determined to keep a cool distance from the students. He thought most of them were boring or obnoxious or just plain annoying. Sometimes Apollo would steal out early with the principal's permission in order to make his daily Narcotics Anonymous meeting where he'd bonded with other addicts in recovery.

A prescription pill popper who logged time in a mental health facility during graduate school, I empathized with Apollo's predicament. Transitioning from, literally, a speedy life to a structured, calm one was difficult. Apollo would talk about how this contrast could be downright disconcerting.

Before class, during snack time, and waiting for his ride home in the synagogue parking lot, Apollo would bend my ear about colleges, benzodiazepines, Clearasil. He'd gush about *Rushmore* (Apollo was a huge Wes Anderson fan and wanted Jason Schwartzman to play him in the movie version of Apollo's life) and offer varying criticisms on such films as *Eternal Sunshine of the Spotless Mind* and the HBO miniseries *Angels in America* (Tony Kushner is Apollo's literary hero). He was also an aficionado of German cinema. "I am thoroughly convinced that Werner Herzog is the greatest man alive," he'd repeatedly exclaim of the Munich-born director, "an incomprehensibly phenomenal human being, and possibly the greatest filmmaker of all time."

Like other recovering teens I've met, he talked about drugs. Apollo loved drugs. He missed drugs. He was addicted to conversations about them. He'd utter sarcastic barbs about rehab and art projects in occupational therapy, and he laughed over how he snoozed his way through mandatory touchy-feely group therapy sessions. And yet, despite his derisive attitude toward rehab and drugs, which for him acted as catharsis, he remained actively committed to staying clean.

More standoffish spectator than gung-ho participant, Apollo made similarly precocious observations on the state of Hebrew elementary school education. He'd poke fun at the staff-organized Purim spiel. He'd mock the parents who got bunched up over their kid getting a B in Introduction to Prophets. "The only thing I've learned hanging out in class," he announced one day over doughnuts and milk during recess, "is that even when a kid is only nine years old, you can *completely* tell what kind of adult that kid is going to be." Indeed, Apollo boldly represented himself as an authority figure on parenting, burgeoning adolescence, and emerging adulthood.

With his unique insights and cheeky witticisms, Apollo acted as my conduit into the thorny world of adolescent boyhood and teen pop culture. He often functioned as a teen culture consultant, even drafting a glossary of terms and definitions.

"Emo" was the name he assigned to cohorts of the teen clique prone to black clothes, weeping, self-mutilation, and listening to bands like Dashboard Confessional and Death Cab for Cutie, which provide veritable anthems for the Emo lifestyle.

"Emo has come to mean something entirely different from what it used to mean," Apollo lamented one day, currying fashionable disdain for the group he was once a proud member of and now was just a nostalgic alumnus. "True Emo is a dying breed. It used to be a lot of emotion. Emo used to be bands like Drive Like Jehu, Three Mile Pilot, Hoover, Jawbreaker, Sunny Day Real Estate, things like that. It was a bunch of guys in San Diego in the early '90s who wore Vans and cargo shorts and shirts that were too big for them and looked all gawky and were really pissed off about a lot of shit. I'm not exactly sure when it turned into bands like the Early November, Taking Back Sunday, Finch, the Starting Line, and stupid shit like that, but the fact that it has disturbs me at, like, a gut level. People don't even know what you mean when you say Emo anymore. They think of fags with their hair in front of their face."

These bands had packed a cultural sucker punch among the current high school crowd. While the elementary school Andy Gibb obsession back in the 1980s spawned count-less decal T-shirts of the *Flowing Rivers* album, it was likely less emotionally searing than iTunes playlists revolving around bands with the words "confessional" and "death" in their names.

Of course, teens who've done drugs and listen to songs with an angry streak in them are not necessarily bad kids. On the contrary, kids like Apollo can be sweet and affec-tionate and enjoy the simple pleasures of life. On the one-year anniversary of Apollo's sobriety, I was invited along as he and a few of his friends in recovery joined up for dinner at a cozy, trendy sushi restaurant in the San Fer-nando Valley. There was Serena, an eighteen-year-old model with tumbling chestnut hair and a stack of silvery bangles on her bony tattooed arms; Miki, a moon-faced boy with spiky blue hair; and Roxanna and Raquel, fresh-faced seventeen-year-olds with long rock star hair and tight little bodies that slid perfectly into Juicy Couture jeans. Roxanna looked like Gwen Stefani, Raquel like a young Pat Benatar. They were both recovering coke addicts.

Apollo and his friends hugged and kissed one another hello. They snacked on salted edamame and sipped foun-tain Cokes as the conversation ranged from 1970s music to current indie cinema ("I fucking *loved* that movie; such an unexpected performance by Johnny Depp") to Amer-ican politics. "Not everyone's politically active but polit-ically *interested* at least," declared Apollo of the crowd at his school. Predictably, invectives against the Bush ad-ministration were bandied about with the sophisticated nonchalance of a college faculty cocktail party. While some may discredit teens as apathetic slugs interested only in themselves, Apollo and his friends engaged in hearty conversation and displayed the intense intellectual passions that many teenagers today possess.

A few weeks later, after I had many phone conversations with his mother trying to arrange some one-on-one time with Apollo, my then fiancé and I treated him to a performance at a Hollywood theater of *Coke-Free J.A.P.*, a one-woman show about a neurotic Jewish Manhattanite ninety-two days sober flinging herself back onto the dating scene.[5] I was reviewing the play for a Jewish weekly and had a hunch that Apollo would take to it.

Sure enough, the show reminded the self-reflective teen of his own painful struggles recovering from crystal methamphetamine addiction: "Drugs are a problem of really highly intelligent people," he uttered at one point during the performance, "and frankly, it's because we're all bored and all the boredom seems like it's palpable that we need to do drugs."

Often Apollo would talk of having so many thoughts swirling around in his head that the result could feel downright vertiginous. No amount of stimuli could provide a creative outlet for it all. The world had become a very understimulating place for him, and drugs seemed a perfect way to dissipate some of the noise. Speed kept Apollo's body awake and moving when it physically couldn't keep up with the whippet-fast pace of his mind.

Throughout the play, Apollo laughed knowingly at the protagonist's casual references to cocaine, her hysterical sociocultural rants on everything from sex to her psychiatrist to SSRIs, and her ongoing frustration over her strained relationship with her emotionally detached father.

It was unnerving how closely Apollo related to the play's sophisticated subject matter. I'd have rested a bit better if he were more naive. But as anyone who's spent time with teenagers knows, adolescent naïveté has sadly gone the way of the dinosaur.

In the spring of the following year, I was teaching at a different Hebrew school and Apollo was no longer my TA. He was finishing up his sophomore year of high school, and we were sitting at a café catching up and talking teen cliques and clans. "Emo is old news," he declared that day, no longer harboring any lingering romantic attachments. For real this time. "I'm over it," he insisted. "I'm moving *on*."

Teens often float between cliques as they try to firm up their identities. Dr. Robert R. Butterworth, a prominent trauma psychologist and media commentator who consults on such troublesome teen issues as peer pressure, contends this habit originated when prehistoric man picked and chose among groups (or was pushed out of them) based on such attributes as physical strength, body type, and an overall sense of virility. Even early Homo sapiens could have trouble fitting in.

"It's quite possible that group clique behavior is genetic," posits Butterworth, asserting a Darwinian link between adolescence and its infamous collective urge to drift together in droves. "We see it in the animal kingdom. Cavemen hunted in groups, and all throughout the ages there have been competitions in terms of strength to see which male could be the one who breeds."[6]

At the café Apollo explained to me that there are two main kinds of teenagers: Old Spirits and everyone else. There is a plethora of subcategories into which even the most label-weary, antisocial teen gets sorted, the "Indie

Fuck" being one of them. Apollo considered himself a member and promised to reveal more about this after he further defined the Old Spirit. This was a necessary trajectory, he assured me, if I hoped to understand anything about indie boys like him. As for the Old Spirits, the bulk category into which Apollo falls, he told me that they are basically "advanced Emos." They wear black a lot, are predictably agnostic, the type of kid to keep a dog-eared copy of Camus's *L'Étranger* in his locker. Old Spirits are messy, inscrutable creatures, with troubles that trump those of any seasoned, hard-living adult. Kurt Cobain is a hero.

The Old Spirits, Apollo explained—and there are a lot of them—can't relate to their often airbrushed portrayals on film and TV. (*The O.C.* with its soap operatic subplots and poster cast for perfect orthodontia doesn't cut it, he told me; it's no wonder the show was canceled.) For Apollo, the staid PG-13 interpretation of the post–junior high crowd as depicted in such films as *Mean Girls* and *Bring It On*, their plots revolving around pastel miniskirts, pom-poms, and designer skateboards, is kid stuff compared with how real-life teen cliques, especially the male-dominated ones, play and act, many of which project, collectively, a striking cynicism shades darker than a Dostoevsky novel.

There are, according to Apollo and other boys I asked, a few notable artistic standouts dealing pointedly with the mad, mad world of the adolescent male experience. *Dogtown and Z Boys*, a documentary by director Stacy Peralta that has achieved a cult following, explores the arena of discarded skate rats in gritty 1970s Venice, California. Stephen Chbosky's coming-of-age confessional *The Perks of Being a Wallflower* muses on everything from mixed tapes to masturbation. *Superbad* provides a comedic look at the emotional bond between two teenage boys dealing with separation anxiety in the months leading up to college. Peter Cameron's *Someday This Pain Will Be Useful to You* has been touted as the current generation's *Catcher in the Rye* (both the Chbosky and Cameron titles provide teen dick lit alternatives to the many adolescent chick lit offerings). Yet sadly, for the most part, teen boys are a demographic that has been jilted in the media.

"You could say the Old Spirits stick together," says Apollo with a long, tired sigh, reflecting on the few boy-oriented films and books that resonate with teens like him. "We've experienced *way* more than we should have."

High school life, per Apollo's worldview, is a patchwork of races, colors, and self-segregating nationalities. From those at the top of the popularity totem pole to those ranking lowest, it's a place where you can label the cultish clusters, all of which, claim Apollo, have had their respective geneses at Emo. "Everyone in this generation was Emo at some point," he confidently states, meaning that all kids have experienced the struggles of feeling misunderstood and isolated, with many of them listening to the moody melodies associated with the Emo movement. "We're all derived from it in some way or another. Everyone had a Bright Eyes phase. Everyone fucking listened to Death Cab, just fucking *admit* it."

At the public high school in Los Angeles that Apollo attends, the teenage tendency to label one another runs rampant. And it's not just the girls who ferociously flock together—boys do the same. "If you go outside during lunch," Apollo told me, "you can literally draw a line down the yard separating all the different groups. On the south side we have blacks and Mexicans, on the north side we have the whites. To be more specific, south for rap, north for everything else. Africa and Disneyland."

This segregating is self-motivated, with students erecting their own cultural boundaries. Said Apollo, teens stick together and stereotype others to maintain a comfort level, based on such characteristics as common skin color, or wealth or religion. Most of this compartmentalization is without racist intent, especially at a big public school where students reflect various cultural backgrounds. Despite the many strides we've made in the way of desegregation, he contended, when it comes to teens, cliques are often about racial commonality. (Conversely, some teens take the opposite approach; an African American boy I interviewed told me he would *only* date white girls: "I'm so *over* the racial stuff," he said to me.) When it comes to racial identity, the main difference today in how adolescent social groups are formed, Apollo told me, is that a teen isn't forced to hang out among friends of the same ethnicity, but, as he contends, in a lot of cases, he still probably *wants* to.

With this in mind, I asked Apollo to describe the most prominent cliques and clans, and he complied enthusiastically, launching into an anthropological ethnography of the lunch hour yard.

He began with brief but biting descriptions of such school assemblages as "the boring kids who study," "the subpopular groups that shop at Hot Topic and will hopefully die miserably in the near future," and "the Goth (at least they think they are; they've never heard of The Cure)." He then fervently delved into more detail, ticking off a litany of teen groups and subgroups, labeling each one almost as if—per Butterworth's apt Darwinian analogy—they were species tagged and classified for taxonomical study.

First off, the Mexican/Asian punks: "One white kid hangs around them too. They don't get that punk was over in, like, 1987, and so they continue to find obscure new stores on Melrose to buy shitty handmade patches of shitty old punk bands that chances are, most of them have never even heard. Why? BECAUSE THEY DO NOT CONFORM! RAAAHHH! Rules to be a Mexican/Asian Punk: No more than .5 square inches on your entire body may be devoid of patch covering (the face may be an exception if needed), must be able to endlessly list bands with similar names that no one has ever heard of, and DO NOT CONFORM! RAAAHHH!" Then there are the Scene Kids, or Scenesters: "They are divided into two subgroups," Apollo explains. "First group: They have big black hair that sticks up in the back and obscures their face in the front, or maybe they have bleached patches; it doesn't really matter. They wear tight black pants, maybe Cheap Mondays or something. They listen to the Blood Brothers, and well, who really cares what else? They don't really have any ideals, and no one, including them, really knows why that started in the first place. They're kind of a dying breed as it is now. They'll either turn into hipsters in the next several years or die out into obscurity. The second sect, in my opinion definitely the preferable one, dresses the same but listens to music like Circle Takes Square, Q and not U, The Number 12 Looks Like You, My Chemical Romance, and shit like that. A lot of them are really just hipsters that aren't old enough yet to fit into that category (I'd say you should hit Hipster at about twenty, but at the least you should be out of high school). Rules to be a Scene Kid: you absolutely *must* have hair in front of your eyes—it must also be choppy and stick up in the back—and hair must be died black, preferably with the back bleached blond-ish, you *must* have tight pants and a tight chick sweater, and a gun belt-buckle is never a bad thing. (A lot of them are ugly fucks, hence the hair in front of face thing)."

Next came the Hardcore Kids: "They wear all black, and they are angry. To give you an idea of how totally awesome they are, here is a list of bands that they listen to (just look at the damn names): Underoath, Throw Down, Avenged Sevenfold, Blood for Blood, Blood Has Been Shed, Most Precious Blood, The Bled, A Life Once Lost, As I Lay Dying (I doubt they ever read the Faulkner book), As They Die, Dead and Buried, Death Before Dishonor, Dead on Impact, Die My Will, If Hope Dies. In other words, they're super deep. And original. They usually have hair like scene kids but without the blond part. They're pretty much just neo-Emo kids gone angry. Rules to be hardcore: Be angry. And be so, so sad. But more so, be ANGRY."

Last was a group to which Apollo referred as "the absolute archenemy of all Emo-derived kids," "the ultimatum of evil," and "the Roy Coen of high school cliques": the Wigger.

Here Apollo drew a mile-deep breath, indicating his loathing for this particular "social sect." "The only thing I can think of that tops my hatred of Wiggers," he slowly exhaled so as not to lose his cool, "is my hatred of Republicans. Wiggers are so uncomfortable with themselves, that they actually feel the need to pretend that they are another race. Which, in a way I suppose means that I should feel sorry for them. But I don't. They wear baggy pants, listen to shitty radio-rap, get cornrows, favor one leg and limp like gimps while holding their pants at the crotch to keep them from falling around their ankles, and speak in Ebonics. Rules to be a Wigger: Be a fucking dumb shit white kid with no self-esteem and some really bad taste in music."

If Apollo's unapologetic and uncensored commentary strikes a chord, it's because we have all been labeled, willingly or not. While Apollo's biases are particularly harsh and he wields language many of us (including teens) wouldn't ("Wiggers," for example, is especially incendiary), in reality such slanderous language is more common than not. Because kids are careful not to talk this way around adults or we're not around them long enough to hear them talk this way, adults don't address this language. Either way, the marked distance we often experience between our lives and the lives of our teens does nothing to help show our kids how deeply problematic this language is. While the terms and titles may have morphed over the years, most of us can remember a period of adolescence when we were lumped together out of sameness or pushed away because we were different. So far out of the loop that we needed a passport just to visit or so far in it that we didn't even know there were other groups *out* there, someone somewhere considered us *something*: nerd, prep, burnout, loser.

From Erik Erikson, who chronicled the eight ages of man, to Amy Heckerling's *Fast Times at Ridgemont High* to MTV's *The Real World*, to Beverly Daniel Tatum's classic book, *Why Are All of the Black Kids Sitting Together in the Cafeteria?* cultural commentators and scholars have investigated this indelicate intermingling of teens in our society as they embark on that ubiquitous adolescent quest for personal identity.

Apollo admitted that group cohesion is one of those inescapable yet madly disconcerting components of the male teen experience. He'd like to be above it all, but whether he liked it or not, this soon-to-be eleventh grade kid was entrenched in the same desperately vain identity search and cafeteria roam as, say, one of his nipple-pierced, spiky-haired nemeses with whom he would have nothing to do. In some respects, no matter what the decade, being a teenage male really is Bowie's "Changes" come to life.

"I don't think it's a stretch to say that no one in high school is really comfortable with who they are," Apollo said with stinging self-awareness, "and that all this desperate clique-searching is really just a vain attempt at trying to define oneself and discover where you'll really end up belonging."

Which is when Apollo finally delved into detail about the subgroup category—under the Old Spirit penumbra, and, yes, he realized that for an adult this can be somewhat confusing to track—in which he *does* belong.

The Indie Fuck.

Rules for being an Indie Fuck, according to Apollo: Have hair in front of your eyes, own at least two band shirts with bands too obscure for anyone but another Indie Fuck to know, have a Livejournal or MySpace account, drink way too much, own *The Royal Tenenbaums* DVD, be "so not-sure-you're-gay it's sad," and listen to music by the likes of Modest Mouse, The Shins, and Elliot Smith (preferably the posthumous stuff).

"I think the Indie Fuck is more the current generation's title for a sect of youth present in every generation," Apollo explained during one of our conversations. "Free thought and the summer of love in the '60s, the KISS kids in the '70s, punk rock in the '80s, Nirvana and grunge and heroin in the '90s, and now the Indie Fucks and the hipsters. We're all just bored, white, middle-class sons and daughters fucking ourselves up because there's not a whole lot else to do."

When asked what might happen if he were from a working-class family that didn't have money and actually had to get an after-school part-time J-O-B (many of the teenage boys I've spoken with didn't have the luxury to sit around bored; they *had* to get jobs), Apollo exhaled a malaise-filled sigh and scratched his stubbly chin. "Yeah . . . If I had to work and actually *do* something maybe it would be different."

Failing geometry is always a plus in terms of Indie Fuck criteria, as Apollo does second semester sophomore year, lectures on isosceles triangles falling mute on ears iPod-ed out on way too much Bright Eyes and Neutral Milk Hotel music. In general, Indie Fucks like Apollo are about as keen on organized education as Howard Stern is on the FCC. Instead, they spend time trying to educate themselves through self-selected books, movies, museum visits, and artistic endeavors in the way of poetry readings and photography exhibitions.

"I was skipping class for a month—maybe *two*?—and all classes except geometry and French," recalled Apollo of his not so banner sophomore year. "We had block scheduling and those were my first periods and that way I wasn't marked absent for the day."

Apollo relished this period of truancy. He hunkered down to smoke butts and read David Foster Wallace novels under the overpass of the 10 freeway. He got really into Wallace's *Infinite Jest*. "It's cool how the main hero loves that nobody knows he's stoned better than he loves actually *being* stoned. I *loved* being fucked up when people just thought I had a really big appetite."

Sometimes he scratched out notes for "The Cons of Patricide," a fictional novella that he was writing about a kid who kills his father and then winds up getting lost in the desert. It's both a sad yet comic story, if slightly incendiary, that explores the perennial themes of loss and restoration, and includes a dad character so out of touch with his son's life that he references Tom Selleck movies as a way to vainly engage him in conversation.

Like Apollo, the novella's main protagonist is Jewish, but, he explained, his "Jewishness" had almost nothing to do with religion. Like many young Jews living in a mostly Christian country, sometimes Apollo felt like a cultural outsider. It's the normal stuff—not having a tree at

Christmas, going to Yom Kippur services when other kids are at baseball practice. Even in Los Angeles with its high influx of Jews, Apollo still felt like a cultural pariah. "I think I mention the fact that I'm Jewish mostly when talking about how I don't belong or how I can't ever fully relate to so many parts of society," Apollo posits, echoing the sentiment of so many other boys his age who just don't feel that they belong.

Loneliness—mostly in the way of lacking a solid confidant—is a theme that runs throughout Apollo's novella, which is punctuated with poetic chapter headings such as "Fantods and Bed Murmurs" and "And Morning Comes in a Lackluster Fit of Obfuscation" and is packed with such cynically trenchant swatches of dialogue as: "I hate to have to promise someone that under no circumstances will I get drunk and fuck someone," or "He's probably one of those guys that can't get hard with the wedding ring on." Saddest of all, because at sixteen he had already developed such a disenchanted view of romantic relationships, "Frankly, if I ever found someone I ever loved enough to marry," he writes, "I would probably love them *too* much to marry them."

"It's my *Naked Lunch*," beamed Apollo of his little novella, which he enjoyed writing above all that school had to offer, which was why he skipped, which was why he kept writing. Until the day he got caught. And he and his family decided that maybe what Apollo *really* needed was a new school situation far away from the whole Indie Fuck influence.

Apollo transferred to a private school. He still considered himself an Indie Fuck, but at his new school the classes were smaller. That meant more individualized attention, and with so few students the clique element was all but gone. "I love it," Apollo said. "I associate with, like, five people, but I love it." The move to a new school suited him as a junior and he excelled in his classes, even getting an A in geometry.

As Valentine's Day rolled around, Apollo decided to break up with his girlfriend and become bisexual. This lasted only briefly. For a few months, he "hooked up" with random girls at parties. "I have come to dislike the term *bisexual*," said Apollo. "Though I just naturally lean predominantly towards the female end of the spectrum, I happen to be attracted to whoever I happen to be attracted to. And that's how I prefer to look at it."

That teenage boys are horny is no Pentagon secret. And yes, many experiment sexually. There's an entire pantheon of names for sexual orientations today, from bisexuality to polysexuality.[7] But the notion that boys are incapable of romantic relationships, as many adults think, is pure chimera. In 2001 Peggy Giordano, a professor of sociology at Bowling Green State University, concluded on the basis of her study that not only do adolescent boys long for true love, but they may be some of the biggest softies around. She surveyed 1,316 teenage boys and girls from the Toledo, Ohio, area and interviewed them about their sex lives. Contrary to public perception, an overwhelming number of boys were emotionally responsive, citing feelings of love and warmth in their romantic partnerships. Giordano's findings concluded that, yes, teenage boys really do have heart.[8]

Surprisingly, it may even be the *girls* who are more sidetracked by sexual longings and fantasies. "Most of the boys I've worked with talk about sex *way* more than they actually have it," agrees Dr. Butterworth, the noted media commentator on boys' issues. Per Giordano's study, the subjects polled concurred that when it comes to heterosexual relationships, *girls* are the ones who want to "do it" more than the guys.

Not that all teenage boys are retiring their Trojans just yet. Apollo talked openly and frankly about the nature of his sexual relationships with young women, admitting that sometimes these liaisons left his adoring mother nonplussed.

One night, Apollo's mother caught him "screwing some girl" at home. She definitely got upset about it, implementing, per Apollo, a decidedly Clinton-esque "don't ask/don't tell" policy. "I can do it in the house but she can't know about it," said Apollo, whose mom confirmed the arrangement. His parents got divorced when he was thirteen and Apollo didn't talk to his dad for a year (par for the course in the world of an Indie Fuck). "I haven't fucked in my dad's house," Apollo reveals, drawing languidly on his cigarette like a character in a Luis Buñel film, "and I have no reason or desire to. So I don't know *what* he thinks."

No matter how common divorce is, it's rarely a party, especially for the children wrapped up in the break. But for a surprising number of male teens that I spoke with who'd faced a family split, it's no catastrophic tragedy, at least not in terms of stunting their emotional development or setting them up for a life of messed up interpersonal relationships.

"Honestly, I would utterly hate to think that my parents' divorce in any way, shape, or form defines who I am as a person," insisted Apollo, exhibiting teenage boyhood resilience in the face of familial disruption. "I find it to be an important event in my formative years, yet ultimately trivial in regards to what and who I am."

Ethan Pollack is a prominent Massachusetts child psychologist who works closely with teens from what he refers to as "families of divorce," a label he favors over "broken families." "There's a temporary disruption for kids who come from families of divorce," states Pollack. "As you might expect, it's a major traumatic event for many kids.

It is a big deal at the time of the event or close to the time of the event. It depends when in time that it occurs developmentally, where adolescence is the most crucial period. But when you look at [children of divorce] over time, most of them manage that and go on and do well. There's about 20 percent who don't. There's a lot more support for kids who are going through it now than there used to be. When you're not the only one whose parents are divorced, when you don't *feel* like the only one, then it takes on a whole different social context."9

Apollo echoed this idea when I talked with him about divorce. "Divorce is no longer a rarity," he affirmed, "nor is it, in my opinion, in any way a tragedy. It is simply society's way of catching up with the fact that very few human beings were ever fit to spend the rest of their lives together. To those few individuals who are, I congratulate and possibly envy them. However, the idea of retaining a marriage once it is evident that the practicality of such is fleeting, if not long gone, merely because it is considered 'right' or 'proper' to do so is, in this day and age, quickly seeming more and more archaic and dreadfully quixotic. People change. And so do relationships."

If you straight up asked Apollo what it takes to be an Indie Fuck, he'd cringe at the implication that a teen can conveniently crack open a preppy handbook–like reference guide to become one. "I almost hate to write a glossary of what I consider to be genuine Indie Fuck because I don't want that to be trivialized," he cautioned.

It's a leafy spring afternoon and we're sitting on the back patio of a coffee shop in Hollywood where Apollo has agreed to meet again and dish further about Indie Fucks. Apollo's hair is in his face, and he's wearing a raglan sweater vest that he filched from a friend. Bright white sneakers have replaced the now totally defunct Converses. "I bought them at Rite Aid for $8," he casually brags. "And these are $125 dollar pants probably, A.P.C." He has a weary look of fatigue in his eyes as he fidgets with his baggy, rust-colored cords and peers busily around the patio for someone with a light, his pack of Marlboro Reds in front of him on the table.

"I don't want there to be an Intro 101 for what I consider to be indie because then we're all gonna have to go out and find even *more* ridiculously obscure things and hate even more of the things that we already kind of like. Like now you don't go to Urban Outfitters anymore, you go to Urban Apparel. Or, I don't know, 'I shop at thrift stores and buy recycled shirts from the dollar bin, fuck I'm cool.' It's like the new indies came along and took away what the true indies started. You're just not true Indie if you're only copying what other people are doing. Being Indie is about being *independent*."

So the so-called new indies are *posers*?

"I hate the word poser," Apollo mutters out of the side of his mouth. "I'd say, like, piece-of-shit-jump-on-the-bandwagon indie kid. You know, they read Palahniuk and, once again, I *love* Wes Anderson, but that's *all* they talk about. And I'm not saying that bands like Neutral Milk Hotel and the Decemberists, both of which I *love*, are not good bands. But it's like Indie 101. Come on, *grow* a little bit, you know?"

The Decemberists, for those *not* in the know, he tells me, is a five-person, Portland, Oregon–based ensemble that has become a veritable poster band for the Indie Fuck generation. Heavy on ethereal instrumentals and dreamy experimental sounds, the group has sold out tours across America.

Colin Meloy, lead singer of the Decemberists, is slightly dumbfounded by his band's so-called indie status. "I usually just call it kind of pop folk music," posits Meloy. "I hesitate to refer to it as indie because I think that's a label that the media has applied and fans have applied to a certain kind of music, and I kind of feel a little out of touch with that. The thing with the term 'indie rock' is that it's not that helpful of a term. It really doesn't narrow it down, even from its base definition—*independent* music—it doesn't really work there because it used to be that indie music was music recorded on an indie label and we are on a major label. I guess it's just a feel of people doing music on their own terms. When I was a teenager, I was extremely proud of the fact that I listened to alternative music—that's what we called it then before it got bastardized by the Smashing Pumpkins and Nirvana world—so I definitely attached a label to it. The thing is, you know, the music that I listened to when I was a teenager and the stuff that shaped the stuff that I make now was music that was enjoyed by lonely, sullen teenage boys, like the Smiths, and the Replacements. So inevitably, I think that's just sort of the way it goes."

Lonely, sullen, and a touch nihilistic. Boys like Apollo have become a bit cynical, at least where modern pop culture is concerned. The music, the movies, the books in which Apollo once took comfort are now being coopted by so many other boys that it's difficult for him to feel like he still has a special and unique relationship with them. For him, "piece-of-shit jump-on-the-bandwagon" has become this generation's "phony." "*Catcher in the Rye* is a prime example of the fact that I will always love that book but it's almost shunned by the quote-unquote indie crowd just because it's been so widely acclaimed and it's easy to get through," says Apollo. "I hate to put it in indie terms, but all the things I'm naming now as jump-on-the-bandwagon shit is exactly what I was doing a year or two years ago. It's because every time people catch on you need to move on, which sucks, because then you end up becoming a pretentious *asshole*."

And yet, at the risk of becoming the so-called asshole, Indie Fucks work hard to fashion a strong personal sense of style not only in terms of music and books, but in clothes. For boys like Apollo, in addition to what one reads or listens to, outward appearance ranks among one of the most vital identifying details. You'll never catch an Indie Fuck going to school in a pink polo shirt with an upturned collar. Just like you'd never catch a Prep heading to class in a pair of ripped jeans.

While Apollo doesn't spend a lot of time on his looks, his *look* is clearly important to him. "I don't shave," he admits proudly. "I don't wash my hair. I get it wet but how often do I shampoo? Once a month—*maybe*. I hate to say it, but I still have a look that identifies me with a group. I think a lot of the jump-on-the-bandwagon kids came on board when they saw an increase in this sort of ragged look around school, and they thought they could just hop into a store and buy the entire look, which honestly is the problem with Urban Outfitters. You want to go look like a fucking standard indie piece of shit, that's like one-stop shopping."

No cookie-cutter Indie Fuck, Apollo searches continuously to expand his knowledge of literature, music, art. Throwing himself into such creative pursuits and hobbies is a source of pride, self-esteem, pleasure, as it is for many boys like him. Most recently, Apollo tells me, he's cultivated an interest in fashion photography. "I really like looking at high fashion spreads and stuff, not that I feel like I could ever pull that shit off, I'm terrible at photography, but I mean, it's kind of interesting just to see how fashion develops. You ever just pick up a copy of *Vanity Fair* and just look at the ads? In last month's *Vanity Fair*, yeah, Kate Moss, there was a four-page Dolce and Gabbana ad, that photo shoot—Oh my God. And I really like—and I don't mean to say this in a weird way—a lot of the nudes in the high fashion magazines. You pick up a *Playboy* and it's like airbrushed and whatever. If you pick up a *Hustler* you know that's smut. But the nudes in high fashion—they're *sensual*."

Apollo is psyched for the release of *Marie Antoinette*. "Marie Antoinette was a party girl that didn't know what to do with herself," he says, blowing a ring of smoke into the air, "it's definitely a period piece, but her predicament of being young and basically confused is pretty current."

Sofia Coppola films, high fashion pictorials, Kate Moss—are *these* the markings of a true Indie Fuck?

"When I think of people who are genuine," considers Apollo, "I mean, obviously there's Indie Fuck music you listen to—I'd say really genuine people return to the basics, like Pavement or the Velvet Underground, Lou Reed and Deep Purple. You can tell people are genuine when they read. When they *really* read. When they read Murakami and they read Nietzsche and they read Dostoevsky. I think a mark of a good indie kid is a good attention span. And you know they don't read Bret Easton Ellis. I like Bret Easton Ellis and Palahniuk—he does his thing, he's like a one trick horse, I've read every single thing he's ever written—but after a while it's just monotonous."

Mostly, says Apollo, being an Indie Fuck is about, well, feeling *odd*. It's about never really belonging. And here Apollo consents—whether you're an Indie Fuck or a Hardcore Kid or a Scenester, most boys, most *people*, are just looking for some way to fit in. *Anywhere*.

"You know," shrugs Apollo, "I think a lot of the genuine people who first became indie—I hate to say the word indie so much—you know, first they became that way when they were eight or nine years old. They were most likely really weird kids, they probably did a lot of weird stuff."

Meloy appreciates kids today falling back on music as a way to soften the blow of exclusion. "I felt really strange as a kid but I think that also had to do with my environment and growing up in Montana and being a kid with kind of leanings toward artful things, you know, doing theater, which in a small town in Montana you're going to be outnumbered by ranchers and jocks and things like that—that was the other boys in my class. As a consequence I definitely felt isolated from them. And because I was shy and kind of awkward I did retreat into music and that was helpful."

But what happens when the "weirdness" and sense of isolation becomes almost acceptable—*popular* even? When more and more teenage boys are searching to dig deep to "discover" their weird side, when being weird becomes pseudo-weird? This is like death to the Indie Fuck. Which is why, in Apollo's eyes, he is being *forced* to move on.

"I hate that people latched on to Wes Anderson," he bemoans. "All the people that still want to be quote-unquote genuine now have to move away from that because they can't be associated with 'jump on the bandwagon' and I still just want to like my fucking Wes Anderson before everyone else gets to him, you know?"

Apollo hates that certain things that were once pure indie are now plain *garbage*. Even if Meloy resists the term "indie" in connection with his band, for fans like Apollo and others of his generation, it's crushing to think that the Decemberists have gone "corporate." This sadness is not just about the music; it's about all of those bygone relics of boyhood that he's torn about abandoning in favor of developing more adult interests. Here Apollo acknowledges that while he hasn't experienced the most innocent childhood on record, it's still *childhood*, with all its sentimental attachments in the way of music, books, clothes. Mixed in with Apollo's desire to mature as he ventures into adulthood is a sense of loss of what he's leaving behind. It's about recognizing that in the future, the things that he and all the other Indie Fucks now love might not be so *pure*. And that means some of the bands, even the ones that were once authentic indie favorites.

"Take The Decemberists and Neutral Milk Hotel for example—The Decemberists' new album, their first album on a major label, is one of the worst pieces of shit I've ever heard," Apollo gripes. "But initially they were great bands. These bands have been adopted as these trademarks. I find it hard to listen to them anymore, and I hate the fact because I hate to be the type of person, 'Oh, they're signed to a major label I won't even listen to them anymore.'. . . now I need to go find bands that are even *more* obscure so I'm not fucking like you pieces of shit. And I hate to feel that way but, like, I don't *want* to be the same as the fucking fourteen-year-old kid with hair in front of his eyes who's carrying a tote bag."

It's been a few months since last we've seen each other and Apollo decides to cut his hair. He's a senior, busy with schoolwork and scrambling to finish up his college applications. His top choices are Reed, Wheaton, Hampshire, and Bard. He's editing his novella and focusing on life after high school. The scruff that used to cover his chin is gone.

If you now ask Apollo about his past use of drugs, he politely balks at the topic. "I just hate talking about it," he tells me, no longer prone to lengthy, nostalgic discussions of his meth days. "To me, it's like playing a sympathy trump card."

These days Apollo is looking for love in mature fashion, opting out of meaningless liaisons in the hopes of finding someone with whom he actually has something in common. He struggles just like anyone else, even if he admits that in his quest to sound more mature, he suspects that some adults will view his commentary as slightly naive. But he's okay with not being taken seriously by every adult so long as he's true to himself, which is also an important part of the growing-up process for boys.

"I feel like I want some kind of companionship," says Apollo with a hint of urgency. "The problem is (I hate to say it because I don't want to say, Okay, I'm mature for my age), but, come on, the average person my age has no concept of what a relationship even is, and I hate to say that I do because I'm still really young but it's ridiculous. Think about how you think of a seventeen-year-old girl and then think of me trying to stay with them."

But the music never dies. Lately Apollo has been listening to a lot of Shoegaze, the Jesus and Mary Chain, My Bloody Valentine, Godspeed You! Black Emperor, Big Black, Beat Happening, Le Fly Pan Am (a side project of Godspeed You! Black Emperor), the Winks, Husker Du, Three Mile Pilot, Drive Like Jehu, Sebadoh, and Set Fire to Flames (another GY!BE side project). "You know," he says, "a lot of big, a lot of post-rock, uh, kinda symphonic sounds, build up, build up, crescendo, build up, build up, kind of formulaic in some ways. One of my favorite bands and I've been listening to them since I was in eighth grade and I love that because I can say I was listening to them way before you were, is Pavement. I *love* Pavement. They fucking define indie. And Stephen Malkmus might as well be *God*."

And what of Elliott Smith, the lugubrious singer-songwriter and secondmost popular poster artist for premature death next to Kurt Cobain? Smith even had a solid run on the pop charts, his music popping up in the closing credits of the Academy Award–winning film *Good Will Hunting*. Even the most unaffiliated of teens spent a month or two courting the "Miss Misery" track.

"I think Elliott Smith will always be in the mix," predicts Apollo, waxing nostalgic for his naively nascent Indie Fuck days. "He stabbed himself in the heart twice. That's pretty hardcore. You want to *die* if you stab yourself in the heart."

But what happens *after*? What becomes of these high school cliques? What happens to the Indie Fuck? Where will they all end up when high school ends, their cliques dissolve, and their old labels go the way of faded yearbook ephemera?

"The search of definition of oneself," opines Apollo. "That's really all this shit is. A search to overcome insecurities, which may or may not ever happen. It's a desperate, vain attempt to become an individual, to do so by finding your personal favorite group of 'individuals.' The punks, no matter how hard they try to *not* conform will just end up conforming with other punks, and most of them aren't intelligent enough to really understand the founding theories of anarchy in the first place, that the only way anarchy would ever really work is if the ultimate goal is a utopian society, a unity of the ensuing chaos once the current global governmental structure has been torn asunder. The Hardcore Kids, and the Scene Kids, and the Hipsters, they're all going to grow up and be semi-cool parents, half wondering if they're just turning into their own. The Wiggers will eventually change, get office jobs, families, and clothes that fit them."

As for the Indie Fucks?

"Oh, we'll be fine," Apollo gently assures me as he affixes his iPod earphones on his head and pumps up the volume way loud on his favorite Husker Du song. "I predict we'll all eventually become semi-happy semi-alcoholic divorcees like our hippie parents knew *they* eventually would."

The
Mini-Adult

I want to say something about maturity. I want to say something about kids in class, about how they act up even though what they are learning in school is helping to prepare them for their future. They do not understand that and they should take school more seriously and also understand that bullying can affect others' learning. Being a part of this book gives me a sense of relief because now I have something in print that's gonna last forever that people can look back on and say, These are my school years, and they can now feel guilty because their bullying is now in ink.

— Maxwell Scheffield

Maxwell Scheffield is the first teen to phone me of his own accord. It's late August and I'm in the hospital, recovering from an emergency C-section. I'm in the midst of a thick Percoset fog, my nurse is checking my vital signs, and my newborn is squawking to be fed.

It's not exactly the time or place for an in-depth conversation about being young and male in America. However, I'm hesitant about letting him off the horn given the track record with some of the kids I've tried to connect with— I'm liable to lose them at any time to football, video games, or myriad other boyhood Bermuda Triangles. But with this particular teenage boy, there's nothing to worry about.

Maxwell Scheffield is *all* business.

Over the phone, the fourteen-year-old peppers me with questions about the publishing world. He requests a faxed copy of the interview release form. He inquires about the book's thesis and about other subjects included in its research database. He asks about the expected date of publication and projected dates for book tour appearances. Will he be on *Oprah*?

When I comment that Maxwell is one of *the* most proactive kids I have encountered in my research, he responds sheepishly, lest he sound conceited, "I'm not one to talk about myself, but . . . *yeah*."

Maxwell next issues a statement that functions as poignant commentary on the ubiquitous loneliness pervading teenage boyhood culture today, his sobering words echoing the sentiment of so many other boys in these pages. "I don't know how I am going to fit into your book," Maxwell professes with a long, weary sigh. "It's tough to relate with other kids. Honestly, not to brag, but I don't know many kids like me."

Maxwell resides in an affluent Minnesota suburb where his parents are partners in a private law firm. He has two younger brothers and two cats. While life's many twists and turns prevent us from meeting in person, Maxwell and I spend countless hours over the course of a year chatting on the phone and exchanging emails.

The "red-haired" teen of "average height" is a generous communicator, candid and forthcoming, and never shy to divulge details or reflect honestly on his young adolescent life. He's also not one to stoop to self-promotion, no matter how "dorky" or embarrassing the details. "I get made fun of because I have freckles," Maxwell admits during an early confessional, "but I could care *less*."

Maxwell's voluble personality is freakishly commanding for a freckly kid in the tumult of adolescence. From the get-go, his assertiveness marks him out among boys. Though he may "care less" whether or not he's mocked for a sprinkling of brownish pigmentation, when it comes to what Maxwell really cares about, the roster of sophisticated concerns and adult-oriented activities are not exactly what many of us consider typical of a teen whose voice is still prone to the occasional crack.

This dichotomy, regrets Maxwell with recurrent twinges of consternation, is part of the problem in terms of how most adults view the current generation of teenage boys. Their range of references limited to the Huck Finn variety of boys plotting mischievous—if not illicit—adventures of all stripes and solids, some forget that there are teenage boys like Maxwell who slip comfortably into the more regimented world of adults. Maxwell's goal, he tells me, in being a part of this book is to prove that he is a living, breathing example of a teenage boy who is conscientious, hard-working, and serious about school and who flourishes when faced with responsibilities.

"I am outspoken," Maxwell declares, "but I feel that I am more mature than others in my grade. I'm interested in some things that only adults really care about. I think in terms of being an adult, meaning at all times I am aware of my surroundings. I *know* what goes on around me. I think like an adult. I *feel* like an adult."

The old soul phenomenon is one that crossed every cultural and socioeconomic barrier as I compiled research for this book. Almost every boy I spoke with said that he felt "old" at least some of the time, as if the world was already a very stale place to be. They didn't look up to adults as seasoned pros who know more than they do. Rather, life experience in the eyes of these boys wasn't about chronology, but about something far more profound. Whether it was Apollo the Old Spirit/Indie Fuck or Maxwell the Mini-Adult—a term he devised to describe the few teens out there like him—they all expressed a sense of growing up before their time.

I spoke with Dr. Ethan Pollack of the Massachusetts School of Professional Psychology about what was emerging

any of the lawyer work, but I take care of all the supplies and the computers."

"Where are the address labels?" In the background on the phone, Maxwell's dad, presumably in the midst of a paper pile-up on his desk, interrupts him. Many times during our conversations, Maxwell's parents chimed in with various office product inquiries—staplers, pens, fax numbers. Maxwell is clearly the one handling the bulk of his family's clerical needs.

"In there," Maxwell tells his dad.

"Where?"

"*There*," Maxwell huffs. He speedily shuffles off for a moment to show his dad the specific spot where he's filed the address labels.

"Today is my catch-up day," he explains once back on the phone, ticking off a to-do list: Call Kodak, Petsafe, Costco. "I called the manufacturer of the boat my family has and got a replacement part because part of the boat was broken," Maxwell casually relates, like it's no big deal, like resourceful teenage boys all over suburban Minnesota are trotting around scoring replacement blow-up pontoons with oars from the manufacturing company *per gratis*. "The oars did not work," Maxwell explains of the little fishing boat his family first purchased. "And by the end of the summer the fabric of the boat, which was red, had turned pink from all of the sun exposure. It was under complete warranty and I arranged for the manufacturer to send us a new one. So, yeah, basically, I got us a new boat because the other one had some rust and other defects."

While other boys he knows dodge garbage duty and eschew household chores, wincing at the prospect of having to meter their parents' mail, Maxwell thrives on such clerical and domestic tasks. This is all part of the Mini-Adult profile, he tells me, performing those necessary—if some-

times banal—deeds from which other kids his age do everything possible to hide.

Even as a small child, Maxwell felt an insatiable curiosity about what he saw adults doing, and he was determined
to do it too. As a toddler, this take-charge temperament occasionally landed Maxwell in trouble—and in *danger*. "I
know how to drive," he informs me one day in a blasé
tone. "I was so fascinated by driving when I was three
years old, I took my dad's car. I backed it out of the driveway. It was fun. I got in trouble but I knew how to work
the gears—I *knew* how to put my parents' car in neutral
because I observed them doing it before. I rolled it down,
across the street, into my neighbor's driveway. I was so
fascinated about that cigarette thing that you plug in. I
was like, 'What is this?' I took it and pushed it and put it
against my hand."

When asked if it hurt, Maxwell briskly responds, "Yeah,
it hurt, and I never did it *again*."

It's early October in 2006 and Maxwell misses one of our
scheduled conversations. A natural presumption would be
that he's off watching the New York Yankees/Detroit
Tigers World Series game. After all, it's the World Series,
and he's a boy. After I leave several phone messages, he
sends a profusely apologetic email. He's had some relatives visiting from out of town, the reason that he was not
in touch. Turns out, I remind myself, not all boys are into
baseball.

What Maxwell is into is personal achievement and
padding his proverbial résumé with the little extras that
will help him get into a prestigious college. Surprisingly,
given what he's revealed of his current tenacity in the classroom, Maxwell wasn't always such an ambitious student.
Maxwell has actually made a lot of strides academically,

he says, from when he was thirteen and didn't try half as hard in school as he thought he should have.

"Honestly I know that I matured a *lot* since last year," Maxwell assesses. "My life has changed. In seventh grade, I had B's and A's and one C. I was not doing very well. I had a 3.2 GPA, and in sixth grade a 2.7. I honestly don't know what changed. I think it's effort, because in eighth grade I *had* to get my act together. I had the realization that I have to know everything in eighth grade in order to be able to succeed in ninth grade, in high school. So I took *everything* seriously in eighth grade."

While other eighth graders focused on forging new friendships and trying out the latest fashion fad, Maxwell was mapping future career strategies. He'd shadow his parents at work, watching as a veritable flotilla of tech support representatives floated in and out of their law firm office whenever a computer crashed, which seemed to happen often. "I watched all my dad's computer guys come in and out of his office," remembers Maxwell of the hands-on learning experience. "He has, like, seven computers so every month probably the server crashes and the guys would have to come to fix stuff."

It occurred to Maxwell that aside from excellent business savvy, the success of a company hinges on its staff's proficiency in all the current technological trends—iPhones, Blackberries, computer software. So Maxwell took copious mental notes and before long he was troubleshooting as well as—if not better than—any IT guy.

Today Maxwell feels confident that, compared to adults of his parents' generation who weren't raised with laptops, web cams, and text messaging in the classroom, he is in a far more favorable position when it comes to parlaying his technological skill set into profitable financial gain.

The entrepreneurial teen—*How to Get Rich* by Donald Trump is among Maxwell's favorite reads—already runs a computer repair company. What started as a side job fixing his family's computers has since bloomed into a modest money-making venture. "One of my jobs today was cleaning up virus-infected computers and making them run faster," Maxwell tells me one schedule-packed day. "I'm teaching some of my dad's clients, and also teaching senior citizens how to operate a computer. What I charge varies from job to job, like $15 an hour to teach a senior citizen how to turn on a computer, to teach them the basics and how to browse the Internet. For computers that need major clean-up and have a virus or are not running up to speed it's more like $35 an hour." Overall, Maxwell estimates he earns about $100 per client.

That many people struggle daily with such computer snafus as spotty Internet service and hard-drive meltdowns and have nowhere to turn save for Geek Squad is a reality that Maxwell finds hard to swallow. "That's not good," he pointedly replies, concern rising in his wisp-soft voice. "I take care of my father's office. I am better than my dad at that, stuff like power tools and computers—I *know* how to fix things. You have to learn computers in order to be a lawyer because lawyers use computers every day. You need to be able to fix it or else your office is going to be down probably for a day or two. And that's not good for business."

Maxwell tells me that he *definitely* wants to be a lawyer.

"Oh, yeah," he confirms in the breeziest of tones. "I'd like to take over my parents' practice."

Maxwell's self-actualization at an age when some parents have to bribe their sons with a ten spot to get them to clean their rooms could strike one as quirky, eccentric, or, well, just plain *weird*. Not to say that Maxwell doesn't want to become a lawyer, or that he won't, or that his aspirations aren't to be taken seriously. But he's still just fourteen. Maxwell *could* change his mind, as do many of the boys in this book about many things, from day to day, week to week. But mentioning this to Maxwell is moot.

"I *want* to be a lawyer," he insists, "or something in business. I don't want to have the type of job where I end up living in a trailer park." I was struck by the extremes that Maxwell associated with not doing well in school, especially for a boy whose parents are successful attorneys. So bent is he on becoming a professional success, he refuses to get weighed down with romance right now or let any active social life jeopardize his making straight A's.

"Boys my age, they want to have girlfriends," Maxwell comments a touch contemptuously. "Right now I don't care about girls. I don't want to get married until I have a good job and I am able to live a fulfilled life and support my family financially to the best of my ability. You're going to have a girlfriend from first grade and then through college and then *marry* them?" Maxwell scoffs. "I don't want a girlfriend that puts me behind in school. I don't want a girl to get in the way of my studies. Which would you rather have? A good-paying job in the future and then have a wife or have a girlfriend from first grade through college that keeps you away from getting a good career because you're spending too much time hanging out? I would rather spend my time getting good grades, getting a good job, get a house and a car and *then* I'll start looking."

For a kid born into the era of Britney Spears, birth control commercials, and Victoria's Secret ads on buses, Maxwell's perception of gender roles rings incongruously old-fashioned. And yet at an age when other swains are swayed by the hot tub and hooters dominating the hip-hop airwaves and MTV videos, Maxwell has a distinctive appreciation for the cerebral qualities of girls. "Girls who show a lot of skin to get a guy—I think that's stupid and wrong," Maxwell vociferously declares.

A profound feature among the boys I interviewed was their tendency toward indecision and changing moods. Maxwell is one of those boys prone to changing his mind. Sure enough, after swearing off the opposite sex in one conversation, in a second one, a week or so later, Maxwell bashfully admits to having a "bit of a crush" on one girl.

"She has humor," describes Maxwell of the girl, "which I like. I've never met a girl who has humor and can socialize using sarcasm. And not take everything so seriously."

When I charge that Maxwell may be the one who seems to takes everything pretty seriously, he balks. "I take things seriously that will affect my *life*," he clarifies. "Like a career."

When it comes to Mystery Girl, Maxwell is waiting to make his move until such time as it doesn't jeopardize his grades. "At school, to maintain a relationship takes away from your studies," he strongly stresses. "I would rather have a relationship over the summer. Once I find the girl who's willing to separate school and social life then I would like to have a relationship. But until then, I'm not going to because I don't want to have to talk to a girl every night for an hour and waste my time."

You also won't catch Maxwell whiling away long hours updating his MySpace homepage or IM-ing with friends as many of his classmates do: "All people do is write stuff like, 'Hi. How are you doing? Nothing much? Bye.' That's stupid and a waste of time. I don't use the Internet to talk to people."

Instead, Maxwell sets his industrial skills to work for his business, or helping his parents, or playing chef for his grandmother's annual New Year's Day lobster fest. "She has, like, a dinner with all her close friends and she pays me to help her cook lobster."

With the money that Maxwell collects from his various entrepreneurial pursuits, he's already amassed a handsome little nest egg, which he estimates in the four-digit range. "I deposit all my checks to save for the future," he proudly tells me. Maxwell doesn't burn any cash on frivolous items like clothes or CDs or magazines or video games.

"Video games are fun but they can be addictive and get in the way of your studies. This kid I know is playing a computer game," he relates disdainfully, "and I'm like, 'How is *that* going to help you in life?'"

Maxwell credits his paternal grandfather with inspiring in him an early sense of entrepreneurialism and exposing him to a beginner's knowledge of mechanics. He was primarily the one, says Maxwell, who molded him into the motivated, budding businessman that he's become. "I really think he was the one who shaped me," says Maxwell. "He was hands-on like me. He owned a business. He liked cars and boats."

Like his grandfather, Maxwell was so mesmerized by household appliances that when he was about six years old—an age at which most parents gift their kids with toy trucks and train sets—Maxwell's parents purchased him a steam cleaner. "I've had three steam cleaners since then," Maxwell estimates. "I'd clean the carpets almost every month in my house for my mom. I was the only one who knew *how* to use the steam cleaner. I've gone through four cameras this year and all have had defects and I have had to return them."

The steam cleaners, the computers, the meticulous obsession with grades. Beyond a recreational interest in gadgets and electronic equipment, beyond an ability to micromanage his parents' office and book their summer vacations, what does Maxwell's unyielding compulsion to fix everything indicate?

In response to this question Maxwell points out that like many kids his age, he is simply a quicker study when it comes to cutting-edge electronic devices that can stump even the most scholarly baby boomer. If it weren't for the high-tech acumen of the current generation, he contends, many American households would be a labyrinthine muddle of extension cords, remote controls, and battery chargers. Maxwell may be a stickler who strives for excellent grades and has a slightly off-kilter proclivity for fix-it tools, but that doesn't change the fact that many of us can't even get the DVD player to work.

For Maxwell, steam cleaning the carpets, arranging family air travel, and gunning for perfect grades is all perfectly normal Mini-Adult behavior—as is watching the news every day, reading CNN.com, and being able to drop the exact figures on Bush's most recent approval ratings.

Four years shy of the legal voting age ("I can't vote, but I still can *challenge*"), Maxwell has already solidified strong political leanings. He shies away from partisan party labels, he tells me, deeming them counterproductive. "I don't believe in labels when it comes to politics," he explains. "Okay, he's a Republican. Okay, he's a Democrat. Okay, but what has he *done*? Not all Democrats think the same way. Not all Republicans think the same way. I never wanted Bush to be our president because his father invaded Iraq and left without finishing the job. I wanted Gore more, but I really didn't like Gore either. But honestly, I wasn't as mature as I am now. I like Gore now a *lot* because of his outspokenness on global warming."

Maxwell blames the U.S. government for mishandling terrorism (immolating criticism of at least some aspect of George W. Bush's presidency came up a lot during my interviews with boys, even among the more politically conservative boys who slammed Bush for escalating the number of troops in Iraq). Like many Americans, Maxwell wonders why more wasn't done to prevent the catastrophe of September 11 from happening in the first place. "We were attacked before," he points out. "I think *that* should have been our wake up call to take the threat seriously and put steps in place to prevent another attack."

At fourteen, Maxwell has lived much of his life in a post–September 11 America, with limited cognizance of what life was like before. Does it all just seem completely normal, or have the more stringent security measures contributed to any collective sense of adolescent panic? Do teens today walk around in constant fear?

"Terrorists are *not* going to bomb my town," says Maxwell. "What are they going to do—bomb a little strip mall? So I feel safe here. I've been to Europe, London—I was there right after the bus bombings. Literally, there were cops that had machine guns hanging from their necks at Heathrow airport. I went to Germany and Austria on a family trip. I was thinking about a terrorist attack on the plane but not so much. I felt safe in Germany."

Ironically, one of the only places where Maxwell does *not* feel safe is at school.

At the start of our long-distance correspondence, Maxwell readies to begin his freshman year at a public high school. He's primed and excited for the myriad challenges and opportunities of a new school, if a little on edge. "High school will be easier socially because I have many more choices in classes," he predicts. "I know other kids who could care less and I won't have to deal with them if I take honors classes."

Like the public high school Apollo attended before moving to a private school, Maxwell's junior high has clique cohesion that demonstrates an ugly, foreboding character. Maxwell and Apollo are not from the same crowd, but their mutual distaste for school groups bears striking similarities.

"There was this group at one table, that group at the other," describes Maxwell of the junior high cafeteria with its cordoned-off enclaves of assorted school groups, cliques that instilled fear in kids who did not belong. "If you sat down at this one group's table they would *definitely* make you feel unwelcome. If you messed with them—if you said one bad *thing*. Those kids were in the majority of fights at my school. Most of the kids that slept in class and copied other's homework, *they* were the ones who flunked most of their exams. They did *nothing*. In seventh grade kids let off stink bombs, these little glass vials that release a fluid with a really nasty smell. I said to them, 'You're hurting my brain from the toxic fumes.' I told them if they are going to do it tell me when and where it's going to happen so I can keep clear of it."

Maxwell agrees that the teen years can be tough on girls as well. He's witnessed some girls making fun of other girls' clothes, peer pressure, and petty cat fights. And we all know from the nonstop flurry of books, films, and primetime documentaries on the subject that girlhood is punctuated by episodes—some lasting for *years*—of seemingly insurmountable crisis. Girls can be cruel, manipulative, destructive, and verbally and mentally abusive. It can feel like being skinned alive to be young and female and simply walking down the high school hallways.

But because of the boys that Maxwell claims affect a brazen machismo, brandishing their blooming physical bravado, flexing the muscles that pop out from under their T-shirts to try and make themselves look tough and impress others, when it comes to surviving middle school the stakes are much, much higher for boys. From an outside perspective, one of the reasons that Maxwell has such a strong need for control when it comes to managing household duties and making sure that everything at his parents' office is in its proper and rightful place is that at school, how the other boys act toward him and toward each other is completely out of his hands. And it frightens him. "The girls are rude to each other," Maxwell compares of how the two sexes fare socially, "but the boys *fight*. They fight if they don't like each other. They fight if they want to show the whole grade who's *boss*."

In middle school, Maxwell was a repeat victim of bullying. "There were kids who bullied me, not just random instances," he recounts. "I walked around watching my back. Kids bullied me all the time, all the time. Their only insult was, 'You're so gay, that's gay.' It didn't make any sense. The kid who just bullied you might be your friend's friend who now *hates* you because you just got his friend in trouble. It was all about popularity. There was no one that I could trust who could make me feel safe."

In sixth grade, one kid tossed Maxwell's semester class project out the window and Maxwell had to get a personal protection order to make sure that the student didn't further harass him (per a 2005 survey, 29.8 percent of students had their property stolen or deliberately damaged by a bully on school property one or more times during a 12-month period).[1] Maxwell was once hit on the school bus, and he made sure the kid was reprimanded. Never a wilting flower, Maxwell has never taken this bullying business sitting down. If you bullied Maxwell, he'd tell on you. If a kid jostled him inappropriately he'd go to the teacher. In middle school Maxwell signed the school's bully pledge, a compulsory document that stipulates if you see someone getting bullied or bullying someone else, you tell a teacher or go ask an authority figure for help.

"Because of all the bullying that happened to me in middle school, I tell my parents pretty much *everything*," says Maxwell.

An estimated 30 percent of sixth to tenth graders in the United States (over 5.7 million) bully others, are victims of bullying, or both. Bullying is more prevalent among boys than girls and the frequency greater for boys in sixth through eighth grades than for boys in grades nine and ten.[2] Maxwell is not certain what branded him a bully target throughout middle school (grades 6–8), but he surmises that it had something to do with his being "outspoken" and "smart." "I put my homework first before hanging out with friends," he says. "All that combined made people make fun of me."

Heading into ninth grade Maxwell can only hope that high school won't present the same menacing atmosphere or discriminating clannish element.

But as Maxwell will soon discover—and what the slightly older boys I interviewed had already learned—cliques generally carry over from junior high to high school. With further distinctions than middle school in the way of honors, AP, college-level, and remedial courses, social grouping has the potential to become even more pronounced, and those yearning for a fresh slate are often out of luck. Even for the most resilient and well-adjusted teen, high school is a trying time, so much energy spent on figuring out what to wear, how to act, whom to know, who to *be*. For some, the experience is downright cataclysmic. For most it can seem like some sick social experiment.

For Maxwell, the paranoia of being bullied in high school is palpable.

"I don't feel popular at all," he admits a few weeks into his first semester of high school, any hopes of starting anew shattered like shards of cheap beer bottles at a Saturday night party. The school is much bigger, there are many more students, and although he has not been physically bullied since leaving middle school, he constantly worries that he will be. "I feel threatened."

Maxwell's fear of high school is mostly residual, common among teen boys who have experienced extreme stress in the wake of past bullying. Maxwell isn't scared of school shootings or knifings or any would-be mass rampages that make the six o'clock news. But he is frightened that what happened to him in middle school—the pushing, the provocation, the mockery—will repeat itself again and possibly escalate to serious physical violence, a sign of how damaging even verbal onslaughts can be to a boy. The way some of the school's burlier boys glare at him, their occasional snarky remarks about the way he looks, Maxwell is afraid that one day one of these kids will take it one step further. One day a band of bullies could gang up on him in the high school parking lot, he fears, their raised fists glimmering with gold knuckle rings. Like other boys in this book who told me they felt terrorized at school, Maxwell's anxiety stems from the nuanced yet brutal ways in which boys can be mean to other boys. So he's on constant watch. "I keep my cell phone on vibrate so I can call 911 if anything happens to me," he tells me. "I *don't* feel safe at school."

When we speak again a few weeks later, Maxwell's spirits have shifted. Like anyone who makes a preliminary judgment based on past experience, Maxwell is now feeling much more positive about the social aspect at school for a few different reasons. He is more acclimated to his surroundings, and he's even branched out a bit and formed a supportive circle of friends that he's met in his honors classes. It's small and intimate, the way he prefers, and he and his new pals share many of the same interests. "You don't need a hundred friends," Maxwell brightly realizes. "Honestly, I just need a couple of close friends that I can talk to about stuff. I have friends that come over before exams and we study and test each other while having fun. They're intimate gatherings, maybe three or four friends. I don't want it to be that big. Because I want to get stuff done. I want to study *and* have fun at the same time."

Maxwell's high school friends run the gamut of backgrounds—Indian, Christian, Jewish. What they have in common is their focus on doing well in school. "I hang around kids who do the work, get good grades, and then have fun, the kind of kids who *don't* fool around in class," says Maxwell. "Most of my friends are smart; they have common sense about what's wrong and what's right—these are people that I met in middle school. If I have a problem then I would tell them. They are all really good friends of mine; they have humor and have a great understanding of sarcasm. They are *all* really nice to me."

But when it comes to discussing the inner workings of high school life, Maxwell remains cautiously guarded.

"I don't want to have anything in this book that if someone does not like they will harm me," he stresses anxiously. "I want to talk to you about how I feel about my life and being a guy and what's going on here at school. I still watch my back, though not as much, just in case a kid comes around the corner and I need to act fast. I won't name names. I have been threatened so many times. I don't want *anyone* to know my name."

It's early December and conference day at school. Maxwell is at home, perusing his latest progress report. He sounds despondent, perturbed. "School's tough," he utters in an exasperated moan. "I'm getting all A's and one B. The B is *really* frustrating to me."

Maxwell's feeling drained from school, from lack of sleep, from the B that he feels is completely unfounded. "I've been pretty mad and pissed off the past two weeks," he huffs. "I've gotten an A in this subject ever since third grade. This is the first year I'm getting a B. In all my other classes I either have a 93 or higher. I strive to get an A in *every single thing*. If I get a B on a test it makes me study more and more for the next test so I get an A in the class. I have to make this long, huge study guide analyzing *everything*. I currently have a 3.85 GPA but I want to do better. I *want* a 4.0."

Despite his determination, Maxwell's fatigue is flagrant even across the telephone wires, his dialogue punctuated by long, intermittent yawns. "I've had this project in one of my classes worth 250 points," he groggily relates. "I was up until four in the morning doing the project. I had many sleepless nights because of this project. One day the counseling office sent me home because I was *really* mad at a teacher. When you're up until four in the morning you know that there's something *wrong*."

Sources indicate that junior and high school curriculums today have a definite tendency to overwhelm students to the point of exasperation and exhaustion—especially the boys—with gender role playing a key part in boys' performance level in class.

According to a recent statistic released by the National Education Association (NEA), the number of male public school teachers in the United States comprises just 29.9 percent of the total number of teachers.[3] According to an article entitled "The Why Chromosome" appearing in *Education Next*, a research journal published by the Hoover Institution, this figure is bad news for boys, as boys who are taught by men do statistically better academically than boys taught by women.[4] (Incidentally, Maxwell's teacher in the class in which he's getting a B is female.)

Wendy Mogel, Los Angeles-based adolescent psychologist and best-selling author of *The Blessing of a Skinned Knee*, agrees that in many respects boys are fighting an uphill battle when it comes to the current high school curriculum.

"The curriculum has gotten so difficult and the central nervous system doesn't mature any faster than it ever has," Mogel states. "We're sort of asking [teens] to be hyper and unnaturally mature in some ways, *academically* for one, giving them a work load they used to never have until college. Boys are compromised and expected to sit still all day and be polite to this person in the front of the room. It's the curriculum that is wrong for boys—the structure of the day, the age at which we expect them to perform academically. It's all *wrong*."

Maxwell isn't the only boy who complained of an unmanageable workload in school. Many teens I interviewed felt spread too thin, having to pick and choose which homework assignments they did because there just aren't enough hours in the day to complete it all. Many, like Maxwell, habitually sacrificed sleep to make homework deadlines. For low-income teens with part-time jobs, balancing work and school was nearly impossible. One boy I met with during the early portion of my research worked the night shift at a fast food restaurant, studying for quizzes and completing his homework when the manager wasn't looking, grease stains blotting his algebra II equations. He'd stumble home at 4:00 A.M., sleep for three hours, then wake up at 7:00 to make it to homeroom by 8:00. This was his regimen four nights a week. Needless to say, his grades suffered. And then you've got a kid like Maxwell who doesn't have to work an after-school job, and he still has trouble finishing all of his class work.

In fact, the stress level among high school students is so steep that school administrations have started to rethink curricula. "The consequences are so great," comments Mogel of the heft in class work and homework assigned to teenage students. "The college mental health facilities are just overflowing. Kids are going away to college that just never used to because of the available medication that regulates their [mental] conditions. They've been so stressed for so many years and at college they don't have their parents there to make sure they're getting to sleep and eat properly—and they *lose* it."

Maxwell's parents think that he pushes himself *way* too hard: "They say it's not healthy for you to try this hard," he tells me, "that sometimes you got to lay *back*." But giving him such advice is pointless.

"Grades count," Maxwell declares. "You should not have *anything* in the way that can affect your grade."

At Maxwell's high school, students who earn a 4.0 GPA receive a commemorative plaque, and Maxwell will stop at nothing to get one. "If I'm summa cum laude and I have that plaque on my wall that says I went to Harvard in my office then it will all be worth it," he says, his inflection flush with dreamy optimism. "Harvard is the only place I want to go. Everything is pretty special if you get summa cum laude."

But there's a force fiercer than bullies that Maxwell occasionally frets will come between him and that special, sanctimonious 4.0—teachers.

"Teachers have a direct effect on my performance in class," Maxwell contends. "It's mostly the older teachers that care less about each student individually. They've been through the school for many years, and it's just another one of those years that they're going to get paid for showing up and teaching the same stuff they taught last year. I have classes with younger teachers in their late twenties or thirties who are very reasonable. If you come in before a test day after school and you are confused, they will sit down with you for hours and hours after school and help you. A teacher who is fifty who's made kids take the same test twenty-five times won't do this."

Maxwell's long-term plan for an educational overhaul?

"Young teachers *in*," he demands, "the older teachers *out*."

There's a heavily trafficked website that allows students to post their opinions about their teachers—www.ratemyteachers.com. Maxwell has logged on many times, using it as a forum to place and review comments about the faculty at his high school.

When it comes to getting that golden grade-A egg, Maxwell is a veritable bulldog in the classroom. Maxwell's bottom line: Just because you're older than me and you're my teacher, doesn't mean you can stand in my way.

Maxwell declines mention of any specific critiques of teachers, but he has stood up to some of them in the classroom. He's lodged vocal complaints about teachers' instructional methods. He's drafted petitions lobbying for school reform. He's penned impassioned letters to the school principal begging for improvements in the classroom. He once tried to get a teaching assistant fired for lack of classroom experience. "Sometimes teachers get freaked out about my outspokenness," he admits. "'You're younger than me,' they say. 'You can't talk to me like that.' But when I think about my career, I'm *not* going to stand around like a kid. I just put a defiant face on. It makes a powerful impression when you act like an adult. You can't be nice if you have been somehow affected, otherwise nothing will be changed. If I let people bully me around I'll never get anywhere. When they treat you like a kid they think they can challenge you in every way, shape, and form and you're not going to respond; you're just going to go cry in your corner. But when they know you'll take it to a higher authority, like the principal of the school, who can help you solve your problems, it's a whole different thing."

Between his clashes with teachers and other boys at school, the bane of Maxwell's high school existence is that he's constantly struggling to find his proper place. Yes, he's made some friends, but he hasn't found his freshman year niche in quite the way he anticipated. Neither in middle school nor in high school does the Mini-Adult truly fit in. Too "old" for most of the students and too "young" for most of the teachers, it's as if Maxwell is wedged in some nether region between the two.

Looking ahead to college, Maxwell hopes to finally secure a spot in that safe comfort zone for which he's been endlessly searching. "The thing in high school is that you are shorter than the teachers," he reasons. "In college you are the same height as the teachers. You are mature enough, you can go up to a teacher, you can talk to them. Intimidation is what is oppressive—if you are intimidated you are *not* going to learn as well."

There are upsides and there are downsides to being a Mini-Adult.

The upside according to Maxwell: "In your head, you act and you see everything differently than others. If everybody sees a car on the side of the road in an accident, they just pass by like they don't even care. If I see an accident in the middle of the road I'll call the police. It's added responsibility. People who are mini-adults are more responsible and think differently."

And the downside?

"You're not sixteen, you can't drive a car, you can't vote. Even though I *know* how to drive a car. I think like that. I *know* how it works, I *know* how to drive. Even though I don't have the same rights as adults I can understand how to do the same things that they do. It's all about your maturity level."

In adulthood, what happens to boys like Maxwell? Many of them, no doubt, prosper financially, raise families, and embark on lucrative careers. Some of them, of course, burn out. Some of them burn out and *then* become successful.

"In adulthood they feel the loss of their adolescence," asserts Mogel of boys like Maxwell. "Adolescence is a very important time to push the boundaries. Boys who don't often feel a rigidity and lack of joy."

And there's regret, and Maxwell knows this.

"Yes, I definitely know that when I grow up I'm going to regret working so hard that I didn't have much time for anything else," he whispers in a hoarse, sullen tone. "But I also know that I will say to myself that if I had been more social and did take more time to talk to friends and did take less time to study then I might not have had my 4.0."

The Optimist

"Zebra Bubble Gum," by Manuel Mejia

School is cool. School slogans, parents, and teachers have tried to convince me that, "School is cool." Much like the rest of the children of tomorrow, I had simply stared upward blankly, smiled, and nodded with a generic smile that said, "I don't understand but I'll comply because I fear the outcome of when I think school isn't cool." As a child I'd walked through most of my life with my hands held over my eyes. Things too scary for my seven-year-old reality were swept under the rug, furtively, by my entire family. A world of crime, troubles, chaos, and bleeding was shielded from my senses. I believed that God loved everybody equally and that bad never happened to the good.

My innocence as a child was marveled by my mother, grandparents, and uncles. They thought if they could control my perception of the world, they could lead me to the "divine path." Grandpa was an abusive, molesting, cross-dressing Indian. Grandma was socially unstable, repressively depressed, and a weekend recruiting Holy Roller. My mom was distant, always working, and insecure. My uncles were recovering alcoholics, recovering potheads, and brilliant artists recovering from lives lived. None of these people had any business leading me toward the stairway to heaven. My influences for growing up were all mixed up and I never had a steady role model.

I grew up in a small town in southern New Mexico and I went to top-notch schools, learning was my number one priority. I had never even heard of a murder that could have affected me personally. I didn't know the names of any liquor or drugs except for beer and the holy spirit. I rode a yellow bus to school every morning. I would sit in the back of the bus with my best friend and laugh through the entire trip because of a smaller white kid sitting in front of us, all alone. Every day we would sit behind the small boy and tell him his mom had died just that morning after he left his house. The boy would insist we were lying and break down into tears. It was excruciatingly funny, and I didn't know why. Pain and death were funny because I didn't know what they really meant. The joke never got old, until I moved to California.

I came into the end portion of my 6th grade year when I moved to Los Angeles. These kids spoke a different language and I only half understood what they were saying. I couldn't find the group to which I belonged because, well,

I didn't belong. I wasn't too rebellious so I chose friends that seemed to be the friendliest. I dove head first into a blur of drinks, girls, and parties. I began to like this fun life more than my life of books and pencils. I stopped going to most of my classes, and found out what my favorite drink was.

By my first semester of my 7th grade year, I had made lots and lots of friends. I liked the lifestyle they introduced me to. I found that freedom was very flirtatious around these times and it begged us all to follow. My friends and I fell into the parties and drugs wholeheartedly, with an unquestioning faith equivalent to that of an omnipotent cult. Some of them tragically became completely overcome and overwhelmed with the lifestyle. I stopped going to so many of those parties after one of my close friends was hospitalized for overdosing on meth.

I attended my first funeral two years ago. My great-aunt died. I didn't know her too well but at the funeral I saw the pain on the faces of her daughter and grandchildren as the casket was lowered into its permanent bed. Then just recently my grandparents' stepdaughter committed suicide after the birth of her child. She had no reason for doing so, but the doctors say it was postpartum depression. My next door neighbor was shot seven times spread out across his back and head as he walked through Venice Beach with one of his friends.

Nowadays, I have a somewhat normal life. I have found that, although one might think circumstances like death and depression might hinder a child's outlook on reality, I believe that they have given me a slighter more aware and exposed view of the world and my world to come. Some believe living is a catastrophe until you're dead. But I chose to not take their word for it. I choose to discover life for myself and never regret any mistakes. For now I can just live a somewhat normal life as a high school student.

When approaching a cliff, stand as close to the edge as possible. The view will be worth the fall.

Manuel's dad is threatening to kick the shit out of him the day he turns eighteen. Manny tells me that he's been planning it with the same ticklish glee as a sixteen-year-old ticking off the days until his driver's license exam. He's waiting until Manny turns eighteen because swinging at a minor is a felony but beating up a legal adult carries only a misdemeanor charge. Manny doesn't think his dad will go through with it (Manny's bigger and stronger than he is), but a gloomy shadow of trepidation hovers above him. Anything can happen when, as Manny reveals, your dad belongs to a gang and is an alcoholic who can't go five hours without a drink else he starts to get the DTs and gets high on crack in the house, when along with the caramel-colored 40 ounce bottles of Miller Lite scattered over the floor, you sometimes find the odd backward-bent spoon with a toasted brown underbelly.

According to a study conducted by the National Institute on Alcohol Abuse and Alcoholism, there are an estimated 9.7 million children under the age of eighteen living in American households with at least one alcoholic parent.[1] Manny Mejia is one of them. His childhood as he knew it came to a crashing halt when he was twelve, as the father he hadn't seen since he was three years old reappeared like a deafening roar of thunder. Since then, Manny's adolescent years have been pockmarked by his father's alcohol and drug addiction, abuse, and gang-related violence.

Most of the teenage boys I've spent time with over the last few years tussled with emotional and physical obstacles—Apollo's meth addiction, Maxwell's perfectionism, and Preston's obsessive-compulsive disorder. Yet Manny's resilience in the face of family dysfunction made it clear that kids dealing with even the most difficult circumstances can develop the skills to take control of their lives and steer them in positive directions.

Manny was not the only boy I met who longed for a loving, steadily employed, at-home father figure of the sort you find nowadays on syndicated sit-coms or Christian cable TV networks. Out of the ten teenage boys profiled on these pages, at the time of our interviews, only three were currently living with their biological father. Roughly five of every six custodial parents (or 84.4 percent) in America are mothers,[2] and researchers have recently noted that boys raised in single-family homes without their fathers are more likely to run away, commit suicide, or drop out of school.[3]

But Manny is determined to beat the odds. Despite domestic hardships, his unflinching optimism says a lot about the potential of boys in America today. Even when life at home is rotten, when there's no steady or dependable guide to help a boy find his way through the myriad rough patches of adolescence, boys in Manny's situation are not necessarily doomed to the same deadbeat fate as their abusive, absentee, or, in Manny's words, "fucked up" fathers.

"I'm not home most times," Manny tells me during our first meeting, cracking a cocked sideways grin that conveys a gut-twisting sadness. "I like to keep a humorous perspective on it, but I *don't* like being there."

Manny looks like he emerged from an all-nighter at a 1970s disco in downtown Manhattan. He's beanpole tall and gangly and his fro is just gigantic. His little sister dubs it the "Man-fro." A mix of Mexican, Native American, and Spanish ancestry, Manny has high cheekbones, smooth mocha latte skin, and amber-colored eyes with flecks of golden yellow. He wears a plastic friendship ring that says BEST BUDS and pastel blue nail polish that his "kinda-like-my-girlfriend" Beatriz painted on him.

"A lot of people at school, especially, in Mexican families, the sexes are really divided," Manny says, spreading his fingers wide so I can get a closer look at his nails. "Men should be men and girls should be, like, girly whatever— it's really weird for them to see a guy in nail polish. It's probably one the things that my dad hates about it. He's used to Mexican people, hard and aggressive and stuff, and I'm not like that at all. My dad has this weird thing with me. I guess he wanted me to grow up in the image of him and I didn't and I guess he's disappointed."

It's a few months shy of Manny's eighteenth birthday and we're at a popular café in the sidewalked Brentwood section of Los Angeles—UCLA students, $5 cappuccinos, and spines of Steinbeck and Kerouac books part of the wall décor. Manny's gritty East Los Angeles neighborhood— far different from Apollo's upper-middle-class L.A. surroundings—is not the kind of place where we should be hanging out after dark, he tells me (I visited there many times before interviewing boys, but comply with his decision to meet elsewhere). "It's cool to be out there; it doesn't scare me," he says, shrugging because he's so used to it. "But it scares *some* people."

At a corner table in the café sit Beatriz, who drove Manny to meet me, and her best friend Laetitia, who came along for the ride. Beatriz is twenty years old and goes to a local community college. She and Manny have been dating for two weeks. They haven't had sex yet (Manny lost his virginity when he was 15). Beatriz doesn't drink alcohol and, although he's never been a hard drinker, as of the weekend before, Manny made the decision to abstain completely. "She's a good influence on me," he says of Beatriz.

Drugs and alcohol are *everywhere*, Manny informs me, and repeatedly refuses offers for free coffee. He used to smoke marijuana but hasn't since middle school. For a while he tried going to parties not to get high but just to enjoy the music and dancing, but one Saturday night not too long ago a street party got out of hand. "It became a real rumble," Manny relates, "like something straight out of that S. E. Hinton book, *The Outsiders*," and one of Manny's friends was stabbed twice in the back. Another one of his friends overdosed on meth. Since then he's steered clear of the party scene.

Manny witnesses the ravaging affects of alcohol and drugs at home. But from what he's seen on the school front, the fallout of recreational use can be just as devastating, because you never know what you're going to get in a hit of one thing or a shot of another. Kids go out looking to have fun and wind up at the end of the night with their stomachs pumped.

If living with an alcoholic dad has taught Manny anything, it's how *not* to run your life. It's not the happiest lesson, Manny says, but a productive one. It's made him sensitive to other teens who don't have proper role models in their world and go out drinking and drugging because they're lost and don't know what else there is to do. Rich, poor, he says, there's a lot of simply "bored" kids out there succumbing to the sordid temptation slithering at every dark corner of the high school hallway.

"Things have changed since a couple of generations ago when kids only had to think about school and home and stuff like that," Manny remarks on the current condition of adolescent boyhood culture—no matter who the boy or from what kind of family. "There's a lot more things to consider. Drugs for one, it's getting *really* common amongst high school students. There's a *lot* of parties in East L.A. There's a lot of drugs."

With his dad functioning as a veritable in-house anti-drug campaign, Manny's actually found a way to turn an obscenely negative parenting example into a self-actualizing one. He stays away from the kids at school who do drugs and alcohol, avoiding the pitfalls to which he sees other boys his age so often submit.

"It's kind of mean to say," he tells me, "but a lot of people think they're my friends but I don't really consider them friends. A lot of them are into partying, like, *really* hard and I just don't like doing that kind of thing."

Jonathan Martin, Manny's eleventh grade English teacher at Euclid High School in East Los Angeles, hands me a couple of personal essays that he's saved in a manila folder in his desk (Manny gives him permission). "In class last year, a lot of the kids had a problem with metaphors or symbolism," Martin tells me, "but Manny seemed to understand symbolism. He has a pretty expansive vocabulary. He has really good comprehension skills. And he shows a *lot* of promise in the way of writing."

Martin's encouragement has been key in Manny discovering a potential career path in life (he's decided he'd someday like to write screenplays) and a creative vessel through which to dissipate life's pain and fashion it into art. "We had a lot of freedom to write whatever we wanted to write," says the now twelfth grader of Martin's nurturing teaching style. "I never really had that before in any other classes. He let me, you know, write whatever I wanted, so I just decided to write my life and it came out pretty cool and I liked it."

For many of the boys I meet, adolescence is a period in which they awaken to the ruthless injustices in the world. Like a cold stab to the heart, rich, poor, black, or white, these boys now have to figure out how to *deal* with it. Like Apollo, whose fiction functioned as catharsis, Manny reveals that his stories too are a literary salve, mending emotional bruises and quelling the pangs of loneliness and alienation that often spring up in his relationships to other teenage boys, and sometimes to the world at large.

"There's just so many fucked up things in the world," says Manny, whose statement recalls the same wounded faith of Apollo, each boy mourning the tragic loss of youthful innocence long before its time. Manny grew up going to a nondenominational Christian church with his family and finds the idea of religion comforting, although at the moment he is agnostic. Manny remains spiritual but he hasn't attended church services in a long time; he doesn't have much faith in structured religion. "I was raised Christian so I guess that's what I am," he shrugs. "And I think about it a lot, because there's a lot of horrible things that suggest there's not a God. A lot of horrible things I've experienced that I probably should have *not*."

Manny's words in his essays bleed like a fresh cut across the page, passages rife with stinging images of a druggie dad who wafts in and out of his life and works odd jobs when he's not in a booze-induced stupor, and of a determined mother who works a low-paying job at a drug and alcohol counseling facility and "pulls money from nowhere" and denies her partner's (Manny's parents have never married) habitual use of narcotics.

In "Rubber Cement" Manny traces his father's vitriolic temperament to a bum childhood on the hard-boiled streets of a rough Mexican border town in southern California, where his own alcoholic father died young and his mother got hooked on heroin; in a twisted familial scenario, she taught Manny's father how to smoke it. "The nightmare that we are suddenly awakened into, like the cold plunge into a lake's midnight hour," pens Manny of the night his father, who one night, screaming high on crack, pointed a pistol at Manny's head. "But, my nightmare is real. My father stands looming above my bed jolting me awake, shotgun in hand."

In "Zebra Bubble Gum," a title inspired by a Discovery Channel documentary on African wildlife, Manny's portrayal of his tragedy-plagued Mexican-Native American-Spanish maternal family tree ("I'm a mix of everything, I'm not sure *what* to call myself") reads like a contemporary Gabriel García Márquez novel, his ancestral brood marred by molestation, suicide, poverty, and seemingly insurmountable grief. An interminable history of alcoholism and drug addiction rips through both his maternal and paternal family lines.

"The zebras represent not being able to fit in," Manny explains of his story, where the zebra is him and the elephants are all the other kids at school with whom Manny doesn't feel he has anything in common. "Zebras have this ability to camouflage themselves within each other, and a zebra in a herd of elephants wouldn't be able to do that."

From the page to present day, Manny openly spills details of the turmoil that has defined the latter half of his teen years.

"I didn't even know who my dad *was*," recalls Manny of his youth in a tiny, quaint New Mexico town where he enjoyed a modicum of tranquility minus his biological father, from whom his mother was at that point estranged.

But like a ticking bomb dumped on one's doorstep, Manny's move to California with his family at the end of sixth grade was a cold dose of gritty reality. "The first night we came over here he just showed up in the middle of the night," Manny remembers of that fateful moment when his long forgotten father stormed back into his life. "He woke us all up and hugged us all. He was real nice at first—I liked him." He smiles wryly at the recollection. "Then he showed his *true* colors."

Since then, Manny has run away multiple times from home, squatting at various friends' houses to escape his father's wrath. He's watched his dad pummel a rival gang member to a bloody pulp, caught him getting jumped in an alleyway, and overheard phone calls recruiting his father to go head out on a hit.

How does Manny deal with it? When his father scolds him or lashes out in an inebriated rage, he simply stands there and smiles. "My dad gets *really* mad," says Manny. "It gets him even more mad because I don't stop smiling."

But mostly, Manny and his father live completely separate lives, which, given the circumstances, is the way Manny prefers it. "He doesn't really talk to me too much," says Manny of their *de facto* tacit arrangement. "Whenever we do talk we're yelling at each other so I just kinda don't talk to him at all. It's better that way."

During the nine years they resided in different states, Manny's father was married to another woman. He and his wife now "hate" each other, claims Manny, but he still refuses to divorce her. For that reason alone, Manny can't understand why his mother would *ever* get back together with his father. "She said that he used to be different," he shrugs incredulously. "I really don't know what to tell her."

Telling her, Manny concedes, probably wouldn't make much difference. "I'm pretty sure she knows what he's doing," says Manny of his father's drug use. His mom has even been known to tote home drug detection paraphernalia—Breathalyzers, iCups, saliva testing kits— from her job. She's tested Manny for drugs even though he doesn't do any. "She makes me pee in a cup," he scoffs of its absurdity—but *not* his father. "I think if all the facts were there that he was doing drugs, I think she would *still* ignore it."

Adults, Manny affirms, don't always want to know the truth about lapses in their own judgment. Sometimes, he says, they like to question their children's lifestyle choices to avoid owning up to their own. Per an item that he posted on his MySpace profile page, Manny often feels that *he's* the parent in the family and his parents are the children: "My name is Manny and i am a stay-at-home mom/dad [i do the job for both of the parents]."

Some may interpret Manny's mind-set as the classic adolescent narcissism of the kind Ethan Pollack mentioned. But other professionals think there are other points to consider. Tom Ross, a retired school adjustment counselor who worked in the Boston, Massachusetts, school system for thirty-five years, believes there is more credibility to Manny's sense of being the "real" adult in the family.

"If you look at the big picture, there is a tremendous amount of adults out there struggling with their own issues," says Ross. "In our world, you try to become the best person that you can be because you can only give away what you have. So many adults can't give that lesson to their teenage sons because they haven't learned it themselves."

Without doing our own soul searching, we can't teach important life lessons to our sons or our daughters. Manny can attest to this shortcoming, having witnessed the struggle of his nineteen-year-old sister who's nine months pregnant with her convicted criminal boyfriend's baby. "I told him don't get caught or you're going to mess things up," Manny remembers warning the boyfriend before he high-tailed it to Mexico to make "fast cash" for the baby by dealing drugs and wound up in jail where he now awaits probation. "'What happens if you get caught? What is the *plan*?' I asked him, and he said, 'I have no plan. I'm not going to get caught,'" Manny huffs. "I *knew* it was going to happen."

Manny wants to support his sister in her decision to raise the baby, but sometimes his resentment makes it difficult. "I was a little mad when she first told me 'cuz that's kind of a really shitty way to live your life," he recalls of his sister's announcement that she was pregnant. Manny doesn't exactly blame his sister for what's happened, or his mom for whatever part, if any, she might have played. He believes that ultimately people possess the power to control their own destiny. But like a number of boys that I met working against the odds to carve out a better life for themselves than the ones into which they were born, standing by as family members make similar mistakes as their own parents can be incredibly frustrating. Manny pushes himself to be sanguine in the wake of familial hard-ships and distractions, but often it's a challenge,

"She wasn't expecting the pregnancy at all and when she called me and told me I was kind of angry at her," Manny admits, "especially with what my mom did with us. She's barely making it as it is."

But where Manny could lash out against his family for the stressful, straining situations he's had no choice but to be involved in, he doesn't. Throughout our many interactions, the teen never cracks once, weathering familial chaos with a buoyancy and aplomb beyond his years. He's determined to spin his sorrow-filled adolescence into a source of strength as he segues into adulthood. Despite everything that's happened, Manny tells me that he considers himself an optimist. He clings to this optimism as a survival tool, as motivation to not let himself get emotionally beaten down. If anything, Manny sometimes worries about *not* going totally berserk. Only once, at a relative's funeral, has he ever actually cried.

"It's seen as kind of feminine to cry so a lot of guys would rather hold it in," he explains, admitting that he'd likely cry more if it were more socially acceptable. Several other boys shared the same feeling with me, their cheeks puffed up with resentment against a social stigma that they stated was instilled by their fathers. Even Manny says this is the only trait he's somehow inherited from his father.

But for the most part, Manny is neither bitter nor self-pitying. Conversely, he's found a way to be gracefully accepting of his family — grateful even. He's not even sure if given the choice he would want a "normal" family, whatever that family might look like, if there is such a thing as "normal" anyway. If he can someday create something lyrical and poetic from the experiences he's had and maybe even make a living from it, then it may all be worth it.

"I think pieces of how I live *are* normal," Manny tells me, folding one of his essays delicately between his palms as though it's an origami arrangement. "Pretty much everybody I know has experience with drugs. And, you know, everybody is exposed to all sorts of horrible things. But I think my family has kinda helped me write these stories. They're the inspiration behind most of these essays. They allow me to write things like this, you know, and let it be the outlet for whatever I want to talk about. And I'm kind of thankful for that."

The red and white walls of Euclid High School are crawling with tales of heartbreak, hopelessness, and defeat. Many of the high school's estimated five thousand students hail from broken or single-parent families, and many parents labor in tortilla factories or as chicken farmers. These are students who bounce around a lot, floating from one city to the next, changing schools once, twice, three times a year. In many instances, it reflects portions of *Always Running*, Luis Rodriguez's candid memoir of itinerant L.A. gang life in the late 1960s, a book that Jonathan Martin assigns in his class. Many of his students have simply disappeared from campus, never to return again.

The difficulty in pinning down teenage boys at Euclid High can be maddening. Getting these kids to talk is the easy part. But after a single meeting and several unreturned phone calls and emails, many of these boys go incommunicado. I spent several hours with a teen born addicted to heroin; his eyes flittered back and forth, unable to focus. Another boy moved so many times and joined his overcrowded class so late in the semester that his teacher had trouble remembering his name.

My second meeting with Manny is on a warm, smoggy day in late November. Manny flags me down during lunchtime where he stands in line at the snack bar on the edge of the school's massive courtyard. Right away he flashes a picture of his sister's new baby tucked behind a plastic photo sleeve in his wallet. He's visibly excited to be an uncle, even if the circumstances are not ideal. He's not too crazy about the baby's name, an outlandish moniker that he fears will trigger years of ridicule in elementary school and beyond, but for the most part he's made his peace with the situation, even if he's still a little mad at his sister. "She always wants to go out," gripes Manny. "She doesn't understand that when you have a baby you really can't have any friends. Even my mother told her that she should have known better. But she didn't listen. She thinks things are going to be different than the way we were raised. But they're not," he predicts sadly edging forward in the line. "She's going to put her kid through the *exact* same stuff that we went through."

Manny buys cookies and a bottle of Vitamin Water and claws his way through the impenetrable clusters of students queuing up in the cafeteria, convening in circular groups to chat and chug sodas and blow off steam between classes. A few kids knock around a basketball. There are boys with blue-streaked hair and silver chain-link belts clinking as they swish around on skateboards, and girls with bangs so stiff with molding gel they look almost shellacked. There are boys with angular hair and deep purple lipstick and girls wearing gold hoops, low-slung jeans exposing fleshy bands of pale stomach.

We pass a pack of "pretty boys" in girlish makeup and hyperstyled hair. Manny looks at them and shrugs his bony shoulders. "Guys nowadays," he scoffs. "We're becoming more feminine than women are what with metrosexuality. People focus on men not crying and whatever, but the truth is, in so many other ways, I think men are losing their manliness, our generation especially. Like guys are, you know, they work so hard to be liked by girls, that it seems like the girls kind of make them fall into one of their 'girlfriend' categories." He looks down at his nails, the polish chipped in places. "And the guys are fine being there."

We find a quiet spot up high on the bleachers overlooking the track and field, the balmy late autumn Santa Ana winds whispering across the dirt and grass down below. It's where Manny likes to hide out during lunch to avoid the crush of kids with whom he generally doesn't find he shares much in common.

"The people at my school, I don't really like to hang out with them," Manny says quietly, picking bits off his cookie. "There's a couple of people that I'll hang out with. I'm not *anti*social, I just don't fit in with most people at my school."

Laetitia and Beatriz are best friends until Beatriz breaks up with Manny to get back together with her ex—who just *happens* to be a good friend of Manny's—and Laetitia and Manny start dating. It's been two weeks and going strong. "Beatriz was my friend's ex-girlfriend or whatever and I wasn't supposed to do that I guess," Manny explains, now squeezed beside Laetitia in a booth in a crowded hipster coffee house in Venice Beach where we meet for an afternoon chat. "There's these certain rules or whatever and I didn't really follow them and he got mad at me. And I didn't want to listen to him and we started fighting."

Where many times dating your friend's ex-girlfriend is an unforgivable boyhood crime ("It's just *so* not cool," comments one boy when asked what he would do if he were in Manny's position), Manny is able to assuage his friend's anger, mainly because he and Beatriz never had sex, and also because Manny is one of those gentle, level-headed, soft-spoken guys no rational kid would ever fight with. "I talked to that guy since," said Manny sweet-naturedly, "and now he's really cool with me."

It's a few days before Christmas and a couple of weeks past Manny's eighteenth birthday, which ultimately passed without his father making good on his threat to beat him up. Maybe he was too drunk to remember that it was his birthday, Manny guesses, or maybe he just got a kick out of threatening Manny and never intended to go through with it. But whatever his father's reasons for pulling back, Manny hasn't spoken to him since.

"I don't hate him," swears Manny. "I can't hate him because he's my dad. If he were another person I'd hate him. He's a horrible person."

Besides his father, Manny now has other pressures to deal with. "I'm really scared," Manny admits, his shoulders tensed up tight around his neck. "I didn't want to be eighteen and become an adult and have to deal with the world. I have to be more responsible—my mom told me to get a job. My mom is *really* influenced by my dad. My dad thinks I should be thrown out of the house by the time I turn eighteen so I'm scared that will happen." He takes a sip of his soda. "And I can go to war," he adds jokingly.

For some boys I met, turning eighteen meant striking out on their own, heading to college with financial support from their parents, mom and dad a mere cell phone call away. But for Manny, because his family can't afford to send him to college and he currently lacks the grades needed for a scholarship (save for English, he's floundering in several courses), being a legal adult really does mean being a legal adult. Not a dependent with a campus dorm address and ATM access to a family checking account. As I discovered, what a boy has waiting for him at the end of his eighteenth birthday is often the variable by which a boy considers himself "grown up" or "still a kid." Manny's not sure what he'll do come graduation in June.

It's not that Manny wants to continue living at home. "I'd rather be living *anywhere* but there," he tells me. But he has nowhere else to go. He doesn't have the money to rent his own apartment, and he knows that securing a decent job without a college degree is going to be a challenge. Still, he holds out hope that his new girlfriend Laetitia can help him figure out his next step.

Laetitia is twenty years old and attends a local Los Angeles-area university. She's pretty, soft-spoken, with a short brown bob. "We were talking, a lot, but I didn't see him as anything," she confesses of a preromance Manny.

A few weeks later and Laetitia is now a pillar of support for Manny, encouraging him to explore avant-garde experimental trance music and study the work of Salvador Dali. On the weekends they go to drug-free dance parties in people's backyards. Already they are "serious." They talk about starting a bakery business together and Manny moving into Laetitia's apartment in East L.A. Later Manny admits, "I think it's mainly that I just want to leave my house. I still share a bedroom with my younger sister." Sometimes Manny and Laetitia spend time with a fourteen-year-old boy from Boyle Heights—a Chicano/Latino district just east of downtown Los Angeles—that Laetitia mentors. The three of them drink fruit smoothies, skateboard around the streets, and watch TV and old movies at Laetitia's place. "I don't think he has any friends his own age," says Manny of the kid. "He drinks too. What he's gone through—it's a *lot* worse than what I have. He starts opening up and crying."

For Manny, it's about perspective. Where he comes from, he's just one sad story in a place where there are many, many others. His being an optimist, Manny tells me, doesn't erase the fact that he's surrounded by people for whom sorrow is a daily fact of life. "It seems like everyone in East L.A. has problems with something," he sighs softly. "It kind of makes me sad."

It's early June and Manny's mother is sitting beside me at a long, rectangular table at the Original Pantry Café in Downtown L.A., a landmark greasy spoon eatery where the line is always long and the eggs are served on little round white plates with butter oozing off the sides. Manny sits opposite us, next to his sickly grandmother who's hard of hearing and looks slightly green under the restaurant's harsh fluorescent lighting.

Manny's mom is here today because she wants to know more about Manny, wants to find out what he's told me that maybe he hasn't told her. My experience as a journalist covering the teen beat and as a teacher taught me that there are subjects about which boys rarely speak with their parents—sex and love the two most obvious. So I found it especially rewarding when a boy and his parents, in connection with this book, wanted to meet on neutral ground and discuss certain topics that they hadn't really explored before.

One of the first concerns that Manny's mother brings up is that of Manny's sexual orientation. Manny's mother was the not the only parent of a teenage boy to suspect that her son was gay even after he'd assured her that he was *not*—suppositions based on choice of dress, close relationships with other boys, and lack of interest in sports. But Manny had never mentioned to me that his mother felt this way so I was a bit surprised.

"I'm not exactly *worried* about him being gay," says Manny's mother, pulling on her long, brown ponytail. "I just want him to be able to *tell* me."

Manny rolls his big yellow-brown eyes. "She's always been really worried about me being gay or something," he says, swishing his flexi-straw around his glass of iced tea. A stack of candy-colored novelty rings covers his fingers today and his hair is twisted up in coarse, frizzy ringlets.

Underneath his hooded sweatshirt he wears a tight royal blue T-shirt.

"I don't know. I saw photos of him dressed up as Wonder Woman for Halloween."

"I just like to scare her," explains Manny of the pictures posted on his MySpace page in which he's wearing bright blue tights and a body-clinging leotard. "I'm not *gay*."

In a culture that still has problems accepting homosexuality and often makes assumptions about people's sexuality based on their fashion choices or tastes in music, it's common for many of us to flirt with the notion that our sons are homosexual, especially if they exhibit traits that aren't conventionally expected of men—like Manny painting his nails. We push boys to form meaningful, long-lasting friendships, and we want them to have confidants they can trust. But if they spend *too* much time with their male friends (and not enough with girls), then many of us leap to the conclusion that our sons must be gay. I repeatedly wondered how this attitude can possibly be healthy for boys.

"The cultural definition in America of being gay is a guy having a close guy friend," proffers Niobe Way. She's witnessed this phenomenon before among boys in her studies. People, she says, often falsely assume that teenage boys are gay just because they have a close relationship with another boy. This can make it extremely difficult for male teens to foster such friendships without feeling that we are all questioning their sexual orientation, an uncommon scenario for adolescent boys who are just beginning to explore their waking sexuality. "It's paranoia," posits Way. "And this microcosm that occurs among boys and their parents reflects the macrocosmic existence of grown males and their friends."

That Manny has a new girlfriend he's crazy about does little to reassure his mother. After all, her own father (now divorced from Manny's grandmother) was a cross-dressing alcoholic who used to strut around the house in tight terry-cloth shorts. He molested Manny's mother as a small child. For "masculinity," that's pretty much her frame of reference. "I don't think he was straight," Manny's mom says of her father, vigorously shaking her head, yet another spoken example of parents projecting their own unresolved issues onto their children. And the boys pick up on it.

"I'm not gay," Manny insists one last time.

"My girls are more like their father," adds Manny's mom. "Manny really is more like I am. He's got a . . . *softer* side."

Manny's mom agrees that Manny might like to dress up like a woman as a reaction to his father's furious displays of testosterone, the three of them now laughing at the visual of Manny's grandfather bare-chested in a halter top and heels. "He drinks almost as much as my dad," says Manny of his maternal grandfather.

As for how much his own father drinks, all three agree: "twenty-four hours a day." But there seems to be some confusion over how often he does other drugs.

"He's not like a *constant* drug user," contends Manny's mom, Manny raising his eyebrows incredulously. "Cocaine, it depends on who's around. He has a cousin who likes to smoke weed."

"He does coke in the house," counters Manny.

"He did it at *one* point," says his mom.

"He did it a couple of days before Christmas."

"And I was there?"

"No," snaps Manny. "You were gone."

Manny's mother struggles as best she can to be there for her children, to encourage them to excel in school and thereby secure a more financially stable future for themselves than she's had without a college education. "I try to tell my kids to graduate from high school and then college," she says. "That's the first step to getting ahead."

But lately she fears that she's spread too thin for time to make much of a difference. "I'm still so caught up in just trying to make ends meet and work," she laments.

"I know I definitely want to go to college or something unless I plan to be alone for the rest of my life," declares Manny. "I'm going to have to support someone so I definitely have to go to college or something. I'm working really hard to figure out a plan. But how I'm going to pay for college and get into college is what I'm worried about right now."

Manny's mother nods her head. "He's very creative," she tells me. "But I also think he's really, *really* unfocused."

A few days earlier Manny received his semester report card, and unfortunately it was spotted with a few Fs. Now, instead of graduating this June, he'll have to attend summer school. "It's kind of my fault for not paying attention," Manny confesses of the flunked courses, which include geometry, which he's already taken twice. Aside from English, he simply doesn't put forth the effort. "I slacked off a lot. I'll do really well at the beginning and then I'll just get lazy," he says. "I do okay on all the tests; I actually get higher grades than some of the people around me. But I never do any homework. *Ever.*"

Yet while he accepts responsibility for his poor grades, Manny also partly blames his parents for their lack of school involvement. His mother, he tells me, has never attended a single parent-teacher conference. "My father could go," he says, "but I doubt I'd want him to."

The guidance counselors at school aren't much help either. "They got their hands full," says Manny of the eight or so counselors divvied up among Euclid's thousands of students. "They don't really have time to give any advice."

When I looked at the boys I interviewed who did well in school grade-wise (including the ones who wrestled with learning challenges) and the ones who faltered, there was consistency across the board: The boys who earned good or above-average grades were the ones whose parents made their children's high school experience a priority — regularly attending school functions, perusing each course syllabus, helping them with their homework.

In her book *A Tribe Apart: A Journey into the Heart of American Adolescence*, journalist Patricia Hersch, who spent six years chronicling the lives of a group of teens, stresses the critical importance of parents being consistently present fixtures in our teenagers' lives — even when they don't want us to be. Hersch discusses how during adolescence our children will many times not approach us on any assortment of hot-button issues — sex, dating, school. But when they *are* ready to talk and we are not around, the resentment can be damaging to teens' sense of trust in their parents and guardians, pushing them to separate from us even more.

"There is a frightening mismatch in America between the lives our adolescents live and the willingness of adults to absorb those lives and talk to teens before trouble occurs," writes Hersch. "The blindness . . . isolates adolescents from freely communicating with adults and locks them in a tribe apart . . . The more we leave kids alone, don't engage, the more they circle around on the same adolescent logic that has caused dangerous situations to escalate. We need to reconnect with them."[4]

While Manny's mother works tirelessly to fulfill a double role as both the mother and father (she's the family's main financial breadwinner), and is clearly emotionally supportive, her not being at home is what Manny somewhat blames for his slacking off at school. Her logging long hours at work has prompted Manny to conceal particular facts about his life from her, such as the friends he's made outside of school, and what he does with his weekends. He has chosen to isolate himself. He sleeps out at Laetitia's most of the time and won't come home for days. "I've pretty much built, like, an entire other life for myself outside of the house," Manny tells me.

It's also the reason that he doesn't often let his mother read his stories. "I don't really *mind* when she asks questions about what I write," Manny shrugs evasively, "but I don't like to address stuff. Growing up nobody really asked me any questions, you know, with my dad and stuff, so it's kind of weird to suddenly, you know, have people asking me stuff."

His mother's eyes well up with tears. She does this all the time when she gets upset about something, Manny tells me, or when she feels inadequate because her children are out of her control. Manny shirks from embarrassment. As his mother blots her eyes with a tissue, he shields his face behind a napkin.

"I just hope he has an easier life," Manny's mother pleads. She draws a long, deep breath and slowly exhales.

Manny's mother feels helpless because she doesn't know about her son's daily life. "I know nothing about Manny," she sighs in resignation, rubbing her watery eyes. "I know *nothing*. I want him to have a good life, but I don't know what is going to happen."

Manny doesn't look at his mother. He bends his straw while staring down at the half-melted ice in his tea. "My teacher Mr. Martin told me all I had to keep doing was reading and writing and it would take me somewhere," he softly tells his mother in an attempt at emotional consolation, pushing to reveal the optimistic side that he hopes desperately will prevail. "Really," he promises with a slight catch in his throat. "It's *already* taken me good places."

The Troublemaker

You've heard the way I live. You don't see people like me living to be eighty years old. I like low expectations because then you don't get as bummed out when things don't work out. When you're sixty and go to the country club—there's nothing to do. When you're in your fifties and sixties you get sick, your body breaks down. I've only lived sixteen years but I have seen a lot of crap. Shit happens. I just want to leave this town because I want to start fresh, get the crap off my back, just get the load off my shoulders. The social worker? She's all right. I meet with her. We talk. It's just repetitive. I pretty much tell her what she asks. I'm pretty open with my parents. But we don't really talk that much. Not about that kind of crap. We don't have any deep conversations. They wish that I would have deep conversations with them but we avoid those. They just turn into arguments.

—*Nicholas Blythe*

Nicholas Blythe pulls down his pants in the parking lot of Panera Bread in coastal Connecticut to show off his bullet wound. It's a faint, raised scar on his upper right thigh, roughly the size of a quarter. It's difficult to tell if it really is a bullet wound—it looks like an old acne scar—though Nicholas swears it's true.

"I actually got shot," the sixteen-year-old brags in a blasé, off-the-cuff manner. "Look at this hole up here on my right leg. I got hit by a stray bullet. No *joke*."

Nicholas pokes repeatedly at his thigh, pressing on the faint pinkish mark.

"I was just hanging out with my friends," shrugs Nicholas of the incident. "We started hearing gunshots and stuff. Some kids were shootin'—I don't even know

as he sits down at the table, giving his thick brown hair a generous toss. "Hey," he says.

I wasn't exactly sure what to expect of Nicholas. Days earlier during a phone conversation, his mother had exhaled a beleaguered sigh and uttered that ubiquitous parental lament: "I don't know *what* to do with him."

Nicholas's mother rattles off a long list of her son's problems that neither she nor her husband nor a family therapist has been able to solve: Nicholas isn't interested in school. He's not goal oriented. Nicholas attends church services and youth group functions twice weekly, but his pastor can't get through to him. Nicholas has become a permanent fixture in the principal's office at school. He's been put on probation for underage drinking and sentenced to community service. He sees a social worker weekly to deal with what Nicholas himself calls "attachment issues."

"I always hated the title 'troublemaker,'" Nicholas self-consciously professes that day at Panera Bread, "but I guess I am one. That's how people think of me. Even my dad says that I'm insensitive to other people. On a scale of one to ten, in terms of attachment, and ten being the least attached, I'd say that ten is me—and dead people."

Nicholas readily admits (and his mother confirms) the following: He does not mesh well with authority figures. He curses constantly and inappropriately. He is impermeable to disciplinary measures at home and prone to volatile outbursts with no easily discernible trigger. (According to his mother, he recently told a friend of his younger sister's, "You're fat. Go home and hang yourself.") Nicholas has no serious plans for college, although he's getting passing grades at the moment (in order to play football he had to sign a provisional contract that he'd maintain a C-plus grade point average). During freshman year he skipped practically every class. He cites both a

Hamlet paper and a health class essay that he's currently avoiding.

Earlier during sophomore year, Nicholas was suspended from school for calling a teacher "a fucking prick." He's been accused of sexually harassing another teacher and flirting with her on Facebook. "I've got this student teacher and she's just a real pretty lady," says Nicholas of the scenario that landed him for the umpteenth time in the administrative wing at school. "I never really did anything. I just sent her a message, 'What's up?' It was like, 'Hey, how's it going?' And then maybe three days later in school I went up to her and asked her if she was ignoring me and she said 'I'm not allowed to talk to you on Facebook.' And then this other teacher grabbed me by the arm and said to me that I'd better watch my boundaries."

That Nicholas has garnered a schoolwide reputation as Connecticut's resident problem child is beginning to get him down. He's fed up with being the go-to poster boy for bad behavior. The cops know him by first name, he claims. He gets pulled over in his car at random. In his mind, he's undeservedly become something of a suburban Connecticut scapegoat. "I'm just going to pull you over anytime I see you because you're just a *shmuck*," Nicholas says an on-duty cop once said to him. And the teachers at school are fast to blame him for every scuffle on campus. He'd like nothing more, he tells me, than to extricate himself from the birdcage that has become his adolescence. But he feels stuck, like he'll never be known as anything *but* a problem child. "I just keep getting screwed over," he huffs exasperatedly. "I'm never going to do really good because anything I do I'm always going to get blamed for it even if I haven't done anything wrong. At school I have to take back roads, just to prevent getting harassed."

But where Nicholas seems to think that it's everyone else sabotaging his high school career, it's what his parents deem a blatant disregard for the potential consequences of his behavior that drives both of them mad. The mounting stress of dealing with Nicholas's wild antics and erratic misconduct both at home and at school has pushed nearly all of his family members to the breaking point.

"He has no judgment," Nicholas's mother says ruefully. Like so many mothers I meet, on one level or another she just can't seem *to get through* to her kid. "His morals are so weird. I truly do not understand him. He'll call me a fucking bitch and actually think we're equals. He'll say, 'I'm trying to speak my mind.' He doesn't see the big picture. It's like he doesn't understand."

Frankly, Nicholas admits, neither does he. Indeed, many boys feel *much* more helpless than the adults around them when it comes to figuring out the roots of their behavior. Talking with these boys quickly reveals that one of the biggest misconceptions about them is that they possess a cognizant awareness of *why* they act the way they do. But scientific evidence about adolescent brain development suggests this is not always the case. When teenage boys act out, so to speak, most of them know when their behavior feels "off" or "wrong." The sticking point, however, is that they haven't yet reached a level of neurological maturity to know *why* they feel this way or *how* to effectively change their behavior. To blame boys without affording them proper direction is pointless.

"Wouldn't that be nice to know," Nicholas shrugs with a self-deprecating smirk of why he acts the way he does, his tone slightly hoarse and deep. "My parents tried to get me, like, counseling and stuff 'cuz I have a weird mentality, I guess. I don't know why, but I don't really have regard for very much. I just don't have any goals. I don't have any *aspirations*."

Most of the boys I met experienced moments of self-doubt but found the courage to overcome them. Nicholas, however, appears so beaten down by what he feels has been stereotyping that he's given up any further attempts at self-improvement, resigned to always being a failure. What I find fascinating about him is that even where Nicholas is struggling in school, constantly getting into trouble and basically making his parents' lives hell, he confesses to me that he still compares himself to other boys his age and feels instinctively that he is above and beyond them in terms of maturity level and intelligence. Listening to Nicholas, it strikes me that there must be some sort of breakdown in communication between boys, because much of what Nicholas says reminds me of my conversations with Maxwell, who with his drive to secure perfect grades, become a lawyer, stop at nothing to achieve *summa cum laude,* feels the same way about kids in *his* life. These tendencies were evident in boys on both sides of the spectrum—those who did well in school and in those who fared poorly.

"I'm a lot smarter than people my age," posits Nicholas without a hint of hesitation or irony. "I just look at kids that are just around me and I just, I don't know, for some reason I just know they're real *stupid.* Even if they are doing smarter things and I am doing stupid things. Even if they've got something that I don't—regard for my future. It still doesn't matter. They're still stupid. High school is a big waste of *time.*"

Nicholas can't pinpoint when exactly the trouble began, but he can trace part of it as far back as the third grade, before the cross-country move to Connecticut, when his family was still living in a sleepy little hippie town in central California famous for its boardwalk, progressive activism, surfing, and weed. "I was just never motivated to do any work whatsoever," he recalls of these relatively sanguine elementary school years. "Pretty much starting in third grade, and all throughout elementary school, I did no homework at all and I passed every subject by getting hundreds on all my tests and quizzes. I can pretty much just sit there and everything comes to me very easily. I've never had to study in my life."

Nicholas's family was itinerant, changing northern California addresses eleven or twelve times during his early adolescence. His father worked at a grocery store until Nicholas was ten, eventually completing an accelerated two-year business degree program at a local community college while his mother juggled parental responsibilities raising Nicholas and his three younger siblings with part-time college courses and a full-time job.

"My dad actually graduated second from the bottom of his high school class," boasts Nicholas proudly, in an attempt to draw a parallel between his father's lackadaisical high school performance and his own, and how it all seemed to work out just fine. "He was a surf bum. But he graduated with a 4.0. Then, after my dad got out of college he started a little business. He's real smart; he just never did anything in high school."

Nicholas's mother confirms that for her son, crossing coasts when he was eleven was a doctorate-level crash course in culture shock. Bounded on the east by a placid bay dotted during summer with catamarans and flashy sail boats, their new hometown was mostly Republican, mostly white, and located in one of the wealthiest counties in Connecticut. Compare all this with the leftist liberal surfing mecca they had just left, with its multitude of bong shops and proclivity for antiwar protest movements, and it's easier to see how, at such a pivotal stage in development, Nicholas lacked a definitive sense of *esprit de corps.* He did not fit in anywhere.

During this period, says Nicholas, is when he truly started to act out.

"The biggest shock was the schools," recounts Nicholas of the switch in sixth grade. "Because I went from a school which was 120 students, real small, like, *everybody* knew each other, everybody was real nice. Then I went here to school and it was, like, *huge*. There were tons of kids. It was middle school but it looked like a high school to me."

Shortly following his family's transfer to Connecticut, however, Nicholas's father lost his job and remained unemployed for the next two years. "That was hard," says Nicholas. "We almost lost our house. Money's been tight."

That he was surrounded by so many rich kids at school for whom cash floated about in excess made Nicholas resent the move even more. "That still pisses me off," he fumes. "But I've gotten used to it. I don't know—just kids that I see that are given *everything*. I like to earn things I have, and I see kids whose parents just hand them out money and stuff. Most of the kids in my school get spending limits for their first cars and most of them are something like forty, fifty, *sixty* thousand dollars. Go to my high school parking lot. You will see Mercedes and BMWs. It looks like a lawyer's firm parking lot."

According to the boys I interviewed, more than race, religion, or ethnicity, socioeconomic factors play a markedly decisive role in creating schisms among teens. "Status matters a lot for adolescents," confirms Robert J. Sampson, Ph.D., chair of the Department of Sociology and Henry Ford II Professor of Social Science at Harvard University. "People tend to sort themselves by similar characteristics, such as by education and social class, a sociological phenomenon called 'homophily,' or 'love of the same.' Increasingly, in terms of marriage and relationships, people are sorting themselves according to socioeconomic background, which means that their kids in high school also tend to dive into cliques by way of social class—as well as other identities. Affiliations tend to be concentrated in sort of a social form and that leads to social influences. It's a fundamental feature of social life."[1]

I witnessed such clustering tendencies in several of the boys I met. Miguel, the "Teenage Dad" in Chapter 9, felt ostracized from wealthier black kids similar to Alain (the "Sheltered One," Chapter 11), and vice versa; Henry Platt (the "Homeschooler," Chapter 10) was homeless with his family and later made to feel isolated and pitied by the experience; Preston Bard (the "Rich Kid," Chapter 7) felt that kids without money jumped to conclusions about him, assuming that his life is pitch perfect just because of his padded bank account.

In talking to these boys, I repeatedly discovered that class concerns are still a huge issue among boys.

Nicholas's mother now works full-time as a bank teller and his father has secured a steady position with a profitable Connecticut-based company. "It all worked out," Nicholas blithely quips, poking fun at his semiprovincial town famous for its summer boating season and nautical Ralph Lauren yachting attire. Nevertheless, the stark contrast between the Blythes' modest middle-class orientation and the surrounding displays of garish wealth play a significant role in Nicholas seeking solidarity outside of the rich kids at school. Later, looking back on it, his mother says that it might also have to do with the reason that he fabricates certain facts about his life. Since there's no way he can live the life of these other kids at school, he works to create an image that's even more drastically different than who he truly is.

"Nicholas gets nothing," says his mother. "A lot of kids here get several hundred dollars a week for allowance. But Nicholas has had to work. In terms of his spending and earning he's got to do it on his *own*."

In several of our conversations, Nicholas ticks off long lists of lies that he attempts to pass off as truths. These fibs are outlandish in nature and packed with chronological inconsistencies. Nicholas relates a string of unnerving incidents involving run-ins with the law, deadly violence, drug addiction, alcohol abuse, and a nihilistic view of life that no sixteen-year-old ought to possess (one thing Nicholas does not fake is his cynicism).

But what complicates Nicholas's mendacity, as I discover through follow-up conversations with his mother, is that threaded within them is factual information as well.

Here is the "truth" according to Nicholas: Starting around eighth grade he got hooked up with an older crowd, a changing coterie ("unsavory characters" is how Nicholas's mother refers to them) that now includes assorted friends and acquaintances in their late teens and twenties. Some of them are the older brothers of friends from school, others are random people he's met at college social gatherings to which he's scored invitations. Nicholas claims that one of his friends is "schizo" and is doing time in a mental institution for trying to kill his wife. Another friend, he says, is in a New York gang. "I always had a lot of older friends because I kind of matured fast," explains Nicholas. At six feet tall and pushing 180 pounds, he passes physically for a young man in college. Hence the ease with which he slides into the local Connecticut party scene. "Like, it's a small town and stuff. I just get around a lot."

Nicholas first got drunk at a friend's house party in eighth grade. With a nostalgic smile, Nicholas recounts all the dizzying, room-spinning details. "The guy's parents went on vacation to the Caribbean," describes Nicholas of the suburban Connecticut after-hours scene. "It was a *huge* house, and there were maybe two hundred people there. I pretty much downed half a thirty rack, like fifteen beers in like an hour and a half. I was *plastered*. I was hung over for a good three *days*."

When asked if his parents took notice or meted out any punitive measures in the way of chaining him to an algebra II book in his room for a month, Nicholas flashes a devilish grin.

"I got home at, like, midnight and for some reason my parents weren't home until four in the morning," he says of that booze-addled night when he supposedly passed out in bed, his parents none the wiser. "My parents know I drink," he assures me casually. "My parents know I do drugs. I'm very open with my parents actually."

The arrest came next, he tells me. "I was just at a party and I was drinking and the cops showed up," he says of the night when the police busted another underage fête he attended, buzzed on beer and hard liquor. "We were actually in the backyard and they came and everybody went to run through the bushes and I was like, 'Fuck, I'll just stay here, I'll deal with the cops. I'm not running through two miles of thorns.' So the cops questioned me. And they gave me a sobriety test, which I *failed*. And then they cuffed me and took me to the police station and called my dad to come get me."

Nicholas started drinking "the hard stuff," he tells me, the summer between his freshman and sophomore years when "a really, *really* good friend" of his was murdered in his apartment. "He was shot, like, five times in the chest," relates Nicholas with accompanying exaggerated hand gestures. "He was twenty-three. I've actually had *nine* of my really close friends die over the last two years."

He's doesn't provide many details of how the other eight died. When I remark that to be sixteen years old and lose nine friends must be a heavy emotional burden, Nicholas represses a lopsided smirk. "I've got some fucked up shit," he reiterates with a long, wistful sigh. "I *do* think of what I'd be like if a bunch of stuff hadn't happened."

He "deals" with it all by drinking. Drinking, he tells me, has always been his primary manner of coping. After his friend was found dead, Nicholas bought a big handle of Absolut vodka. He downed it, he says, in a single sitting. "I drank vodka when I was depressed," he says. "I just drank a lot. I would pretty much drink myself to sleep. I have addictive tendencies and an addictive personality."

At one point, a friend suggested that he attend a few AA meetings. Nicholas went but didn't get much out of it. "I thought it was kind of retarded," he guffaws dismissively of the experience. "First time I went there I sat down next to this older gentleman, he was like forty-two and he goes, 'What are you here for?' I said, 'I think it's kind of obvious, I'm in Alcoholics Anonymous so I drink too much.' Then I asked him what he was here for and he tells me, 'All these alcoholic girls got low self-esteem so I take them home and sleep with them.' No joke," scoffs Nicholas. "I mean, this guy's a junkie and a *half*."

Nicholas also regales me with tales of habitual cocaine use. Coke, he says, is easy to get at school; it's a "rich kid's drug," so everyone has it. "I do it as often as I can," he declares, pressing his palms hard back and forth against his faded jeans. "I've actually been caught with drugs in my car by the cops. But I don't do it *all* the time—it's a money thing. I have stolen money to buy coke, but I try not to do that. I saved up a lot of money doing work over the summer. I have almost a thousand dollars in there. I went through six hundred bucks once on cocaine."

Nicholas *loves* doing coke, he exclaims with unfettered ebullience. He's not high now, he "promises," but he *will* do coke this week, probably right after this interview. First chance he gets he's going to score an eight ball from a guy he knows at school. He's not scared of overdosing. He's not banking on sticking around long enough in this life to collect any social security checks. He's not, Nicholas assures me with morbid clarity in his voice, in any way scared of death.

"My mentality is like I'm going to die eventually," he casually declares. There's something markedly detached about Nicholas's sense of mortality, a submissive acceptance that has ripened the proverbial fruit of youth far too early. Other boys were pessimistic in certain moments of despair, but their skepticism eventually gave way to optimism. Yet throughout every interview with Nicholas, he made it clear that he feels life is pointless.

"There's nothing to stop me from dying today or years from now," he pronounces rather indifferently. "I've seen a lot of deaths so I definitely don't feel invincible. Death, in that way, just never bothered me."

When he was fourteen years old, Nicholas came close to death. He was mugged at gunpoint and then he found God—or at least this is what he tells me.

"I was walking to my buddy's house," recounts Nicholas of the encounter, "and I stopped in at the 7-Eleven to get a soda and a guy came out and mugged me. He had a gun to my head and he was real messed up and stuff. He was drunk. I got two big Slurpies and he actually put a gun to my head and shoved me up against the wall and said, 'Give me your money.' I do kind of have trouble with people pushing me around and stuff so I was just like, 'I don't have any money just leave me alone, freak.'"

That's when the guy pulled the trigger. "I was scared shitless," recalls Nicholas of that first loud click in his ear. "I'm a massive guy but I almost shit in my pants. I was like, 'Don't kill me.'"

But no bullet fired.

When the gunman pulled the trigger a second time, Nicholas started to pray. "I was sitting there praying," he says. "I always thought like in my last minutes I'd be praying 'cuz, I don't know, I think about that stuff."

Nicholas was brought up a Christian but insists that up until that moment, a gun pressed against his temple, the fact that he attended Sunday morning church services was more rote than anything spiritually inspired. The Wednesday after-school youth group he now "reluctantly" frequents is a place where Nicholas bemoans, "I really don't fit it at all with any of the other kids." They're boring homeschool kids, he says, virgins, profiles that don't exactly jell with Nicholas's ceremonial deflowering at the age of thirteen to a sixteen-year-old in the backseat of her Jeep.

"Relationships are for people who plan on getting married in the near future and I don't," he makes clear. This attitude, of course, generally doesn't mix with the squeaky clean-cut kids at church who haven't so much as French kissed. "I was never really into it that much," says Nicholas of his Christian upbringing.

Nicholas's admission reflects the viewpoint of most of the boys with whom I spoke. Religious affiliation was generally casual, by way of familial association. If their parents were Christian, they considered themselves Christian (Manny). If their parents were Jewish, they identified with Judaism (Apollo). While approximately 90 percent of contemporary American teens are affiliated with a religion denomination, few of the boys I met were zealots.[2] Their religious involvement hinged more on celebrating the cultural traditions of their faith, such as spending time with family during major holidays, partaking in social events at their local house of worship, and attending supplementary Sunday school because their parents signed them up. If religion was important to these boys it was primarily because of its cultural, traditional, and sociological aspects. Many of them were still undecided on whether God exists.

Nicholas insists that he was one of these kids until the gunman pulled the trigger a third time and still no bullet came, then turned around and ran away and left Nicholas standing against the wall behind the 7-Eleven—*alive*.

That was the moment Nicholas first truly believed in God.

"I've seen some people survive some shit that they shouldn't have survived," he tells me. "That's why I go to church."

Nicholas's mother refutes much of what Nicholas says as twists on the truth, creative falsehoods spun out of desperation and frustration. Nicholas was never arrested at a friend's party (although he was caught drinking and sentenced by a local judge to community service). He was never held at gunpoint. And he never went to AA. "He just says that to be funny," she tells me. "I don't know why he says that to people." And while she can't prove that nine of Nicholas's friends *haven't* died, she's only heard of one, a homeless boy he knew peripherally who was found on the streets beaten to death.

Nicholas's mother knows that he's never spent $600 on cocaine, at least not if he withdrew the money from his account. She works at the bank where Nicholas has an account, and she checks his balance almost daily, so she knows exactly how much he withdraws and when he spends his money.

As for the religious epiphany that drew him back to church, the truth, she affirms, is that Nicholas has always been an active and enthusiastic member of his local congregation, regularly placing among the top in interchurch Awana Club Bible verse competitions. He was once crowned champion. "He's got a brain that just absorbs," says Nicholas's mother of his proclivity for memorizing biblical passages. "He's got a vivid imagination. He started out very shy, very timid, and now he's just outspoken. He's got an incredible vocabulary. He's just a very dynamic kid."

Nicholas doesn't lie for the sport of it, his mother insists. He does it, she explains, because he doesn't trust that anybody—not his teachers, not the school principal, and at one point not even his parents—will listen to the ordinary truth.

The litany of behavioral and emotional problems that Nicholas has experienced over the past few years—the lashing out at teachers, the irritable mood swings, his constant use of incendiary fighting words—have prompted his high school faculty to peg him as a drug addict. They did so because they failed to come up with any alternative explanation for his behavior, and, like many of us, associated drug use with "bad" kids who exhibit blatant disregard for authority. And while Nicholas's mom doesn't doubt that Nicholas smokes marijuana "occasionally" and that he once sampled coke, that he's a recurrent hard drug user is a pack of lies. "The truth," she affirms, "is that he talks way more than he does. When he is on drugs, he always says something. But drugs are *not* the real problem."

That Nicholas's behavior has remained an enigma to many people has led him to fictionalize particular details of his life to match the skewed image that folks at school have grown to erroneously expect of him. When they peg him a cocaine addict, he'll make up crazy stories about a night spent drinking and drugging that never happened. He does this, posits his mother, to accomplish a sense of triumph over those who have failed him.

"They don't understand it, how to deal," laments Nicholas's mother of the teaching faculty and, in particular, the high school principal. She's tried to secure help for

Nicholas, but it's been nearly impossible, she asserts, to get the school on her side. "They are making my life difficult. Just always saying, 'He's on drugs.'"

Swayed by the school, Nicholas's parents have had him drug tested—blood and urine—by his pediatrician on several occasions. Nicholas was so miserable during one of these tests that he was pushing to drop out of school. "He tested negative for *everything*," says his mother. "Out of the five times he's been tested, only one test came back positive and it was for pot."

That Nicholas's parents took steps to rule out suspected drug use created a temporary strain in their relationship. Even if they weren't outright accusing him of doing hard-core drugs, they had him tested, and this made Nicholas feel that his mother and father were siding with the school and not him. Says his mother, "We're realizing that things we've done even when we've had him tested for drugs, he actually felt that we were choosing to believe that he's a drug addict."

Of the night that Nicholas "stumbled home drunk" in eighth grade, the events did not unfold as Nicholas describes. His parents were at home and scolded him appropriately, and for the next several days nursed Nicholas's raging hangover. "He probably did have alcohol poisoning," says Nicholas's mother. She also admits that while after that night Nicholas occasionally did get drunk with his friends, his drinking doesn't tell the whole story. Rather, since the onset of puberty, she has suspected that Nicholas's drinking obscured a far more complicated problem. He drank, says his mother, because he felt like he was slipping away from himself, and the booze helped dissipate his out of control mood swings that no amount of disciplining or talking to seemed to quell. "He definitely was a vodka drinker," she says, "but it was really because he got sick and nobody could figure out what was wrong with him."

In an effort to decipher and treat Nicholas's troubling misconduct, his parents have taken him to see numerous adolescent psychiatrists. Over the past few years Nicholas has been professionally tested and evaluated for bipolar disorder, attention deficit hyperactivity disorder (ADHD), oppositional defiant disorder (ODD), and depression. In order to find a therapeutic and stabilizing course of medications, he has been prescribed several stimulant drugs such as Adderall and Concerta, both of which are typically prescribed for patients with ADHD, the symptoms of which include inattention, hyperactivity, and impulsivity.

It's not an uncommon scenario, as boys are four times more likely to be diagnosed with the disorder than girls (percentage of girls 3 to 17 years of age ever diagnosed with ADHD, 5.9; percentage of boys 3 to 17 years of age ever diagnosed with ADHD, 9.5).[3]

"It took a year to get him to a psychiatrist," recalls Nicholas's mother. "I had to keep canceling because he simply refused. You can't lift a 6-foot, 180-pound kid and put him in the car. He thinks there's nothing wrong with him. He finally went, '*Fine*, put me on drugs.'"

But as many parents of children with psychiatric disorders have experienced, getting Nicholas to the doctor's office was the easy part. Securing a proper diagnosis was infinitely more challenging. Given the lack of an infallible litmus test for mental illness, determining its genesis and an effective course of treatment can be as dizzying as the disorder itself. Ever more frustrating for parents of teenage boys issued an alphabet-soup of diagnoses such as ADD, ADHD, and ODD, is the inscrutable crossover between them. Parents such as Nicholas's are left to sort through the labyrinthine letters while trying to decipher the most therapeutic ways in which to help their children.

It takes several sessions with his psychiatrist before Nicholas is diagnosed with ADHD with "signs" of ODD. According to the American Academy of Child and Adolescent Psychiatry (AACAP), ODD affects 5 to 15 percent of all school-age children. Its many disruptive symptoms include recurring and unremitting patterns of uncooperative, defiant, and hostile behavior toward authority figures, frequent temper tantrums, and excessive arguing with adults.[4] Its causes are not fully known, but genetic factors are thought to play a role. Since there's a history of ODD-like behavior on Nicholas's mother's side, she says that the diagnosis "makes sense in light of getting information."

Demitri Papolos, M.D., director of research of the Juvenile Bipolar Research Foundation and coauthor with Janice Papolos of *The Bipolar Child*, further explains why securing a proper diagnosis for teens such as Nicholas exhibiting symptoms of psychiatric disorders requires intricate and careful analysis. "Our own studies have shown that over 90 percent of symptoms that are used in our current diagnostic nomenclature (DSM-IV) to diagnose ADHD overlap with BPD," Papolos explained to me. "Using current diagnostic standards it can be difficult on clinical grounds alone to differentiate between the two conditions. However, family history of bipolar disorder and a specific set of symptoms should allow clinicians to make the distinction." He adds that "several studies have reported that over 80 percent of children who have early-onset bipolar disorder will meet full criteria for ADHD. It is possible that the disorders are co-morbid or that ADHD-like symptoms are a part of the bipolar picture. Also, the ADHD symptoms may simply appear first on the continuum of a developing disorder."[5]

By May 2007, on medication to treat both ODD and ADHD, Nicholas still had rapid cycling mood swings, and his psychiatrist additionally diagnosed him with bipolar disorder and started him on Depakote, a mood stabilizer often prescribed for patients with the illness. (When treating neurological disorders, a positive response to a medication is often an effective diagnostic tool.) "We're going to look at the aspects of bipolar disorder," his mother explained of the mental illness that affects some 5.7 million adult Americans (ages 18 and older), and includes symptoms of distractibility, poor judgment, drug abuse, and extreme irritability.[6] Like ODD, bipolar disorder has a genetic link. Says Papolos, "While no exact link to one specific gene has been found, it is more likely that the disorder will be found to be caused by a number of genes that produce a susceptibility. In addition, most clinical studies would suggest rates are *much* higher in boys."

Nicholas's family *finally* witnessed encouraging changes in his behavior once he was taking Depakote. "It's helping," said his mother, her voice laden with noticeable relief. "His temper doesn't last as long. He's not as reactive. At first when he started the drugs he said he felt like he was intoxicated. After that he was *fine*."

If Nicholas's ordeal can teach us anything, it's that we should not necessarily blame ourselves for all of our children's problems. Nicholas adamantly states that he's never done anything for the sake of rebellion or to strike out against his parents and neither, he suspects, do most teenage boys. As he comes to terms with having a mood disorder that requires medical intervention to control it, he wishes that he could strip away the pain and scourge that he has heaped upon his entire family. "My mom is the most amazing lady in the whole world," Nicholas lovingly gushes. "I couldn't do anything without my mom."

When Nicholas's mom reflects back on the challenges of raising her son, she credits it as one of life's greatest learning experiences. "At first I just thought it was puberty," she jokes. "But now I understand him more and know that you kind of have to coach him through everything."

Together, Nicholas and his mom are searching for successful ways to manage his condition on the school front where, despite his diagnoses of ADHD, ODD, and bipolar disorder, he still battles a bad reputation that he can't seem to live down. His mother is working to secure an IEP (individualized education process) for Nicholas, which would afford her open access to all progress reports and unadulterated communication with his teachers. She's also applying for a Section 504, which protects all students in public schools from being discriminated against based on individual disabilities. For example, with a 504, Nicholas would have the right to be alone in a different room if there's a teacher with whom he just doesn't get along. "We now know that with ODD there are automatic triggers," says Nicholas's mother. "Certain teachers could cause automatic agitation. A 504 would give Nicholas a safe place to go."

While Nicholas still experiences moments of frustration when he considers dropping out of school, his mother's outlook remains cautiously positive.

"I am hopeful," declares his mother, who believes that her experience raising Nicholas can educate other parents with boys who have undiagnosed behavioral disorders in a society rife with misconceptions about teenage boy behavior. "But it's so hard. Because once you're labeled in the school system there are *no* second chances."

The Gay, Vegan, Hearing-Impaired Republican (If He Were Old Enough to Vote)

> On average, I'd say the majority of male teens today aren't terribly comfortable with their identities, and they don "costumes." But I was actually pretty comfortable with my identity when I realized I was gay. I mean, all I had to do was lay on my bed and finally say, "I'm gay," associating myself with the word for the first time. And then, a moment later, shrugging and saying, "*Cool*."
>
> —*Christopher Erikson, IM message*

Christopher Erikson describes himself as "a gay, vegan, hearing-impaired Republican." And not *necessarily* in that order.

When I initially contact the high school senior from rural Nebraska (we correspond via Instant Message, Christopher's preferred method of communication given his hearing loss), it's late December and he has just completed a six-week seasonal run with a local improvisational theater company that performs skits, scenes, and monologues exploring issues faced by gay, lesbian, bisexual, transgender, and "straight allied" teens (heterosexuals who publicly support gay rights).

"The whole production is essentially about combating intolerance and promoting GLBT issues by presenting them with humor in a variety of skits," Christopher writes me of the teenage drama troupe he's belonged to for the past two years. "We're very open about things, and approach a wide variety of topics, so it isn't necessarily just gay pride, but pride for being who you are, *whatever* you are."

If boyhood pride had a poster teen, then Christopher Erikson might just be it.

Christopher is a politically conservative animal rights activist who defies gay typecasting at every turn, debunking the notion that all gay youth are sexually confused, emotionally dysfunctional, flaming, politically liberal pundits wearing fishnet stockings and wielding giant rainbow flags atop gay pride parade floats while anxiously awaiting the second comeback of pink spandex leggings. And Cher.

This is not who Christopher is at all.

Instead, the University of Nebraska–bound student ("It's close enough that I'll still be at home, but far enough that I won't be *stuck* at home") more closely resembles the type of unabashed modern gay youth that psychologist Ritch C. Savin-Williams describes in *The New Gay Teenager*.[1]

"The field has so pathologized gay youth, claiming that they're depressed, suicidal, radicals, leftists, anything and everything," Savin-Williams notes during an interview, "and the reality is extraordinarily different. Like anybody else, there are some gay teens who are depressed and some who are unhealthy and some who are confused. But most are just ordinary adolescents and they just want to live their lives. They are not any more outlandish than other teens, and they want the same kinds of things that *all* kids want."

Firsthand experience has taught Christopher that Savin-Williams's evaluation of gay youth is true. "Most gay teens are just ordinary adolescents whose only significant difference is who they love and who they're attracted to," Christopher asserts. "Usually it's the most extreme or abnormal cases that we pay the most attention to."

He refers to the infamous 1980s gay Richard Gere rodent rumor as an example of such radical polarization. "I recall there being an instance several decades ago where a

gay man died because he and his partner were having sex
that involved putting hamsters up his ass," Christopher
tells me, unaware that this seminal "news" story was the
work of a whirlwind of tabloid outlets in the 1980s that
pegged the rising movie star as a homosexual with a penchant for bizarre sexual experimentation. When informed
of the truth behind the rumor, Christopher exclaims, "No
doubt many people after hearing that thought, 'Oh my God,
all gay people must get off by shoving rats up their asses!'"

Christopher also refutes the presumption that just because he's gay, he *must* be a bleeding heart liberal who
lobbies to endorse gay rights referendums, and that the
second he turns eighteen he'll become a registered Democrat. He takes issue with some Republican legislation:
"I disagree with the Republican vote when it comes to
giving a boost to animal industries and pushing not quite
so gay-friendly laws," but when it comes to matters like
economic growth, national security, and social welfare reform, Christopher informs me that he would "definitely"
vote Republican. He would have voted for Bush in 2004,
he pronounces. About the Iraq War and the Republican
Party's support for it, he declares, "I don't support war in
general, but it's wishful thinking to assume that we could
ever end it just like that."

In discussing such political leanings, Christopher readily defends seemingly contradictory viewpoints that may
not fit with what most people expect of the "textbook"
homosexual teen in America. "Gay *and* Republican," he
muses. "Well, I don't usually consider the two to be mu-
tually exclusive, except that Republicans are generally
considered to be more reserved about the 'liberal ideologies,' and homosexuality usually tends to be seen as such.
But Republicans can disagree with other Republicans on
some points and still be Republicans. I would say my

political opinions vary, but I side with Republicans more often than not."

Per all of the above, Christopher could easily be regarded a rare and dynamic breed of teen with an extraordinary set of passionate interests, a worldly sense of humor, and complex political opinions. But like many other adolescents, he also possesses his own set of personal challenges: he was born with a hearing impairment of unknown cause.

"Technically, I'm profoundly deaf, although I lie just within that classification on the charts," he writes during our first round of instant messages. "We really don't have any idea why I was born deaf, and in the vast majority of these situations, that tends to be the case."

At school, Christopher works with a sign language interpreter to help decipher his teachers' instructions (he earns above-average grades). Although talking on the phone can be an option with people Christopher has known for a long time, it's generally frustrating for him. We try speaking on the phone, but it's difficult for Christopher to understand me, so we switch to IM mode, where his thoughts can flow smoothly and unhindered. "When it comes to people I don't know," he explains, "I tend to get really flustered and the conversation goes *nowhere* because I have to keep asking them to repeat what they said. Lip reading is half the equation when understanding people, which explains why phones are so infuriating."

Christopher also admits that when it comes to making new friends, it's disconcerting and disappointing for him to see to what extent his hearing aid can be an immediate detractor. "People like security," he speculates. "I have to deal with people who *immediately* stop talking to me and walk away, or treat me like an idiot when they realize I'm wearing a hearing aid. It's amusing sometimes how patronizing some people can get. But I suppose I've gotten as used to it as I can get. Now it's just life."

Yet Christopher has also discovered, he tells me, that being deaf can be a blessing, and he has actually found a way to turn erroneous public perceptions about him on their head, using them to his advantage. "I get shielded from the most intensely shallow people," he lists as one such perk. "As I sometimes get thought of as 'one the disabled kids,' I've noticed that in our society it's not cool to make fun of people like that. I don't have a lot of experience with people bashing me because I'm gay, and my hearing impairment might have something to do with that. Those who do approach me are those who wouldn't be inclined to believe those misconceptions about deaf people anyway, so I get a 'purer,' if you will, crop of friends."

Some people, he tells me, actually want to be his friend *because* he's deaf. "They're curious," he comments with derisive humor, "or they know my name even though I don't even talk to them because I'm 'the deaf kid.' Like a new spring accessory. 'Deaf and gay is in!' 'I'm friends with a deaf, gay kid!' And a gay, deaf, politically conservative vegan kid to boot."

Of the so-called pure friends in his circle, 95 percent of them, he estimates, are girls. "I really don't know why more guys don't talk to me," he professes, "just that there are far more guys who are awkward around me and don't want to talk to me when I'm sitting next to them. I must appear really freakish to other boys because even if they're friends with my friends and joined our group, they don't talk to me. Maybe it's because I'm hearing impaired. The girls, for whatever reason, don't seem to mind as much."

Like many of the other teens I spoke with—mini-adult Maxwell, indie Apollo, and Nicholas the troublemaker—Christopher tends to feel isolated from boys his own age, often finding it impossible to relate to them. It's not because he's deaf or gay that he and these boys lack common ground, Christopher insists, but because, in his estimation, they are simply less sophisticated. "People my age annoy me," he bluntly announces. "They're just less mature than myself."

Like other male teens, Christopher often experiences periods of profound loneliness. While the theater group provides an opportunity for Christopher to express himself through the characters that he plays and engage with other actors during performances, when it comes to life unscripted, he often clumsily stumbles when interacting with other boys. And like a lot of boys, he can't exactly seem to figure out how to rectify this predicament. "Probably a part of it is growing up and going through the stages of becoming an individual," he posits of why many boys his age feel so out of place. "Once that happens and you start focusing on how different you are, everyone else seems that much farther away. Of course, no matter how I try to describe why I feel lonely, no explanation really fits. I'm a loner. In some respects, it just comes naturally to me that I'm just more of a people watcher than someone who mingles. Who knows? Maybe it's me. Maybe *I'm* the one out of touch with boys."

I ask Christopher if he believes that the loneliness he experiences is more intense than the loneliness of the typical teenage boy, and he balks at the suggestion. While he agrees that he has "more things to justify the loneliness if he feels the need to," most boys, he states, on the whole, are universally linked by their sense of having trouble fitting in. It doesn't matter, says Christopher, whether they have a physical disability or whether or not they are gay. In fact, the motivated, loquacious, razor-sharp, occasionally sarcastic seventeen-year-old is living testament to the fact that not every gay teen is sad or tormented or confused simply *because* he is homosexual. Per Christopher, every boy has a part of him that brands him as an outcast.

"I think that on some level, everyone has a freakish side that they don't think anyone will understand," Christopher proffers, "unless you're deluded. I mean, seriously, how many people think they're Barbie-perfect with nothing incriminating under the surface if all their secrets were shown to the world?"

Christopher came out when he was thirteen years old.

"Initially, I dwelled on it in relative isolation," he reveals of the lead-up period to his decision to tell his friends and family that he was gay. "On a certain level it's because I'm deaf and am already a little isolated. Not totally isolated, but somewhat. So it was that and, in addition, it was the fact that I'm just not a social butterfly to begin with."

First thing he did was e-mail a couple of his friends from school. "Word spread amongst them, and that was that," says Christopher matter-of-factly. "Then I told my brother before he was going to bed, e-mailed my sister, and several days later, after one of my theater performances, came out to my parents by saying, 'Mom, Dad, I'm gay.' Then I walked away. A bit cowardly, but it seems to have worked out fine."

Of course, when he tried to kiss a straight boy in the middle of the crowded hallway at middle school only a week after he came out, it didn't go over so well with his parents. "It landed me in a shrink's office and on Prozac," he recalls.

It's not that his parents (now legally separated, a topic Christopher will later discuss) thought that medication would reprogram him à la *Clockwork Orange*, assures Christopher, but like many parents upon first hearing the news that their son is homosexual, they were definitely a little nonplussed, especially when Christopher's untrammeled hormones got the best of him by the ninth grade lockers. They figured, says Christopher, that a psychiatrist was the best person to help *them* deal with it.

"My 'rents were still pretty freaked about the whole gay thing and me kissing a boy at school," he explains of their reaction, "so I guess they didn't quite know what to do."

Christopher stopped seeing his psychiatrist after a couple months and, under that same doctor's supervision, stopping taking the Prozac because he strongly felt that he didn't need it. For Christopher, living in an area of the country where tough, macho cowboys on horseback are icons and a large majority of the population are God-fearing Christians, being openly gay has sparked a surfeit of ideological arguments among his close friends and family. As Christopher puts it, it's a long way from someone supporting you in your lifestyle choices to actually *believing* in them to ultimately grasping that they are not *choices* at all, but as much a part of your human fiber as the color of your eyes or hair. While his close relatives all love him, Christopher tells me, and respectfully tolerate his homosexuality, they have not been shy about lodging moral objections to sexual diversity.

"My grandparents were and still are a little iffy about [being gay]," says Christopher, "yet they insist that they still love me, no matter who I am."

While his father got used to things relatively quickly, Christopher's mother, a born-again Christian, was torn between her religious beliefs and a desire to be emotionally present for her son. "She was a little awkward with the homosexual issue early on," recalls Christopher. "There was one instance where she was crying and asking my sister why I was 'doing this' to her.'" Christopher managed to handle his mother's temporary heartbreak in stride, optimistic that it would pass, which it did. "Since then," he tells me, "she's pretty much gotten used to it and we even joke about the subject."

His evangelical friends from school have maintained a compassionate and warm attitude toward Christopher, even if their church dictates that homosexuality is a sin. "When some of them first became aware of the fact that I was gay they were like, 'Oh, hell no! But my *church* says . . . ,'" Christopher recalls with a twitter of contempt. "But, you know, since then we've all gotten to know one another better and my being gay isn't generally a huge issue. They're very nice people."

Savin-Williams believes that broad media exposure of GLBT issues today contributes to a more viable atmosphere of tolerance among teens of one another's sexual orientation, right-wing Christians included. "The world of teenagers is so similar in rural Nebraska as in Manhattan in the sense that they're often watching the same TV shows and they're logging on to the same Internet sites," posits Savin-Williams. "And I think that's important. Being gay is not perceived as a bicoastal thing anymore—it's across the board."

If anything, states Savin-Williams, teens lead the way in terms of increased social harmony among people of divergent sexual leanings, their vocal tolerance helping to discredit the presumption that human sexuality is a clear-cut black-and-white issue. "There are a lot of kids out there who have same-sex attractions, desires, romances, and not *all* are gay," points out Savin-Williams (as in Apollo's brief bisexual exploration). "I think we have to keep away from our little categories of gay or straight. Adults have problems understanding that boundaries are fluid."[2]

Christopher concurs with Savin-Williams's encouraging assessment. "This reminds me of the Kinsey Scale,"

Christopher tells me, "which labeled most people as bi-sexual rather than as exclusively homosexual or hetero-sexual.[3] In the short story that I read when I was coming out that someone suggested called, 'Am I Blue?' where all gay people suddenly turned blue (the gayer, the bluer), most people were a light blue or something close to it. It taught me that exclusive classifications of 'gay' and 'straight' are misguided. Humans are really too complex to peg down true absolutes."[4]

But even if devout Christians in his inner circle now fully accept in a decidedly altruistic love-thy-neighbor manner that he is gay, it's the mixed-bag reactions of some of these peers and relatives toward issues of homosexual-ity in a broad sense that have subsequently hardened Chris-topher's outlook on particular aspects of society, namely religion, whose tenets he finds can be transparently hypo-critical. Many of the boys I spoke with expressed disdain for hypocrisy within religion, and they favored more prac-tical, all-inclusive approaches to life that don't discrimi-nate against certain segments of society. Most of the boys—even the virgins I talked with—were open-minded when it came to the subject of sexuality, possessing a wide-ranging understanding about it that was far more sophis-ticated than many of us had at their age.

"As far as I'm concerned," reveals Christopher with a tinge of characteristic sarcasm, "most established religions believe I'm condemned to eternal torture. Golly, that just makes me giddy. I'm also thoroughly unimpressed with var-ious churches' attempts to 'modernize' and do youth out-reach. And I am definitely not sent into spasms of joy when I hear otherwise kind and compassionate people say that, 'Why, yes, we love you and welcome you, as Jesus did . . . even if homosexuality *is* a sin.' The combo deal on sin is a nice gesture, but I think I'll pass on joining their church."

Christopher hasn't believed in God since elementary school, long before he came to terms with being gay, and even then he only entertained the possibility of a deity, regarding most of the teachings of the church as "nonsense." He has no interest in becoming moody and bitter over people's faith-based beliefs, however, perceiving most misunderstandings about people a result of simple and preventable ignorance. "I'm pleased to say that I've improved when it comes to how I think about religion," says the self-directed teen. "I've gotten my feet wet with actually taking the time to learn a little about religion and educating myself with books on the subject, so as to better understand where these people are coming from. As much as I get mildly amused and annoyed with people capitalizing the 'H' in 'Him' when referring to their supreme deity, I'm also highly irritated when other people intentionally lowercase the name 'God' and put it in quotes. It's just rude and malicious to go out of your way to reduce a belief system you know almost nothing about."

Like most boys prone to streaks of indecisiveness, Christopher stumbles now and then firming up any concrete viewpoints on God versus Man, but for the moment he is quite comfortable remaining slightly cynical while at the same time continuing to question theories about religion. "I'd say I'm an atheist-leaning agnostic," Christopher responds when asked how, ultimately, he would label any religious or spiritual beliefs. "After all, what do we humans know? If a God *does* exist, there's a high chance that we have all the facts screwed up given all the different beliefs out there. If *no* God exists, then we look pretty foolish right now, don't we?"

His parents, whose marriage, says Christopher, was "strongly encouraged by the church," separated when Christopher was fifteen years old.

"I've been encouraging their divorce ever since I was around fifteen and my dad first moved out because I could see that they just weren't in love anymore," Christopher tells me, "but they haven't gotten around to finalizing their divorce yet. My mom's never gotten anything done with lightning speed."

Like Apollo, Christopher's reaction to his parents' split has never been that it's a catastrophic situation. He wasn't devastated by the news, and his resilience in the face of change has been incredibly instrumental is his dealing with their separation.

"I guess it's about acknowledging the natural progression of things," reasons Christopher with equable calm. "All I know is that I don't regard it to be a big deal, although that's probably just the kind of person I am, but more likely it's just that I don't mind at all. No denial, no hidden issues. Whatever happens, happens. And I respect them all the same. There's really no sense in being legally bound when you haven't been in love for decades. Their marriage was pushed on them by a church—another reason religion doesn't always make sense—and they realized that they didn't love each other shortly after they were married. But they stayed together for the kids. Which is silly 'cuz they knew they didn't love each other."

Of course, he concedes, sometimes the mistakes that adults make yield propitious results. "I know I wouldn't have been born if common sense prevailed," he consents with a smiley emoticon when he writes me by IM, "so I suppose I'm glad people don't make sense."

Christopher seems unflappably levelheaded and practical. Whether it's on the subject of his parents' split or his sexuality or his hearing impairment, he seems to possess none of the dark, twisty neuroses we often associate with the teenage years. Is he sure that he's not suppressing some deep-seated emotional trauma, doing the whole boys-don't-show-their-emotions thing?

In response, Christopher remarks that when we think of boys as emotionless, we're overlooking the more flagrant and pressing reality of how laissez-faire our entire culture has become. All of us, he contends—girls, boys, women, and men—have become equally more *passive* in our relationships to other human beings and, especially, in the way we treat, and mistreat, the earth's natural resources. It's one of the factors that motivated Christopher in his fight against animal cruelty.

"We all live in a passive culture," he laments. "Many concerns revolve around inward things, such as having the best Nike shoes. There isn't really anything in the way of caring about true revolutionary movements."

Many people become active in causes, but in Christopher's experience, they quickly lose interest, giving up out of sheer laziness or moving on to the next "it" movement without any genuine compassion. It's one of the reasons that, aside from the theater company, when it comes to gay rights activism, he's skeptical of self-professed crusader types. "Crusaders annoy me," he says. "For me, it's kind of like they've taken the idea and turned it into a fashionable thing that's cool to campaign for. I mean, it's awesome to see support, especially in the straight communities. But then you see others that *appear* to care, but it's all for show—they don't really have their full heart in it."

His heart fully invested in vegan-related causes, Christopher, who deems himself an "antimaterialist," talks at great length over a period of several months about his rigorous efforts to raise awareness of the inhumane treatment given to many animals in our country. From his school-wide campaign to provide more veggie meal options in the high school cafeteria ("The point isn't really to convert

kids, just to make it easier for those who already have")
to his efforts revamping the once disbanded Nebraska Vegetarian Society to his high-profile role managing protests
for a local veg*n group ("means both vegetarian *and*
vegan," he explains of the asterisk) Christopher has become something of a local vegan hero, even if he is not, as
he explains, "interested in heroics." He even has a pair of
vegan running shoes that are glue free (glue is typically
made with connective tissue from cow hooves and pig ears,
he tells me).

"I became a vegetarian first, and then a vegan for moral
and health reasons," he explains of his journey in cham-
pioning animal rights. "About being an animal lover, I
once heard someone say, 'You say you love flowers, and
yet you pick them. You say you love animals, and yet you
eat them. I fear the day when you say you love me.' The
idea of eating dead animals, even without knowing how
they were treated, didn't sit well with me, even when I
was a very young child. Veganism just feels right, that's
really all I can say."

His parents, maintains Christopher, have been tremen-
dously supportive in helping him seek out a variety of
vegan food options, even if they have some reservations
about a vegan diet. After all, though separated, they both
still reside in Nebraska, a state with a sizable meatpacking
industry and where, Christopher informs me, cows out-
number humans. "If they learned to use guns," he jokes of
Nebraska's bovine population, "they could stage a takeover
any day now."

Christopher's favorite vegan foods include soy milk
and quinoa, Earth Balance vegan buttery spread, vegetable
stir-fry, pancakes, and hash browns. "I think one of the
reasons that my mom and dad have lightened up about
my veganism is that I've actually been noticeably happier
since changing my diet—and have kept getting *taller*."

Five others tried before Christopher to persuade the school to include vegetarian options on the lunch menu, but he was the first one to succeed. And yet, despite his philanthropic determination to make the world a safer place for animals and the beneficent changes he's thus far instituted, Christopher occasionally has doubts about his abilities as an effective leader.

One of these low self-image moments occurred recently, he tells me, at a local KFC, where Christopher and others from the local veg*n group were protesting the restaurant chain's abuse of chickens, wielding PETA (People for the Ethical Treatment of Animals) signs that were provided as a show of solidarity.

"Someone came up to me with a fancy video camera during the protest," Christopher recalls of the scene, "and he was smiling when I fumbled my answers, and now I'm a little nervous that the footage will be used to incriminate me and the cause. It was a bit unnerving. I'm afraid of the idea that my fumbled speech and inadequate answers will be used to make fun of PETA's campaign, giving people more of a personal reason to laugh and reassure themselves that there's no reason to be concerned, whilst they bite into yet another chicken leg."

I assure Christopher that he probably sounded far more eloquent that he thinks and point out that, regardless, some of the staunchest carnivores have a soft spot for animals, so it's unlikely that his comments will be publicly maligned. The boys I interview who possess deep convictions about a particular issue are virtually immune to genteel offerings of adult consolation when they truly feel that they've "messed up." Similarly, Christopher responds to my consoling remarks by asking when was the last time *I* messed up on TV while brandishing a PETA sign?

"When you become dedicated to a cause," Christopher notes, "I suppose the last thing you want to do is damage the cause through your involvement. I suppose I just need to calm down and not worry about it, though."

Animal rights aren't Christopher's only concern. He also worries about love. Like any other teenage boy, for Christopher, figuring out romantic relationships doesn't always come easy. His high school dating life hasn't always been punctuated by puffy heart etchings in notebooks and love letters folded inside math books. In fact, some of his sexual experiences have been tinged with great regret.

"Many of my 'relationship firsts' weren't pleasant at all," Christopher sadly confesses of the string of loveless sexual encounters that occurred during the early years of high school. "I don't mean awkward or embarrassing, I mean flat-out nauseating, because I was—and still am—disgusted by the guys I did them with. I only did them with them because I was lonely, even if I was only fourteen and fifteen at the time. I guess I call it temporary insanity."

I think back to all the other boys who experienced pangs of loneliness—Apollo, Preston, Manuel. And while some may conclude that fourteen is a little young to be sleeping with guys you don't even like because you're lonely, it's become quite clear to me that teen boys, like all of us, struggle to feel a sense of connection with the world. We all want love. We all want companionship. We all want romance.

"I saw these guys to be disgusting because of their looks, their crude demeanor, the fact that some of them were *very* skinny, various body odors," details Christopher. "It wasn't pretty. I had to take a bath every time after getting home. And yet, I don't know, apparently some gut instincts were overridden by 'at least I'm not alone,' even though I was *still* lonely."

So desperate to feel a connection with someone, Christopher admits that he's never worn a condom, prioritizing unfettered (and spontaneous) physical intimacy above self-protection. So far, Christopher has not caught any sexually transmitted diseases. "It's dangerous, I know," he admits, a bit embarrassed, "but the only times I've been with people, it was their first time too. Or if not, then they hadn't been with anyone else for at least a year and were tested for STDs. Doesn't make it entirely safe of course, but there's that *margin* of safety. But I plan to use a condom the next time I do it."

At seventeen and in his last year of high school, Christopher hasn't given up on love. He's working on making smarter relationship choices and, like Apollo and Preston, for whom finding the right girl is crucial in developing a meaningful romantic relationship, Christopher holds out hope that the perfect guy will come along. "As for having a boyfriend right now, I wish I had one," he tells me. "But that doesn't mean there isn't a guy that I *like*."

This "guy" possesses all of Christopher's sought-after traits: "Cute, sensitive, funny when he means to be, and big on academics, which I suppose makes him more likely to talk to me since I'm not a stranger to that."

While they don't talk very often, they do flirt occasionally between classes. "We used to call ourselves 'boyfriends,'" Christopher explains of their brief, undefined pseudo-courtship that happened a while back, a relationship that he longs to rekindle afresh, "although we didn't really date, and that only lasted a month. We only kissed once in a while; it was more like sitting really close to each other and just being comfortable with that. You know, simple things that mean a lot more than they seem to. It sucks too, because then you've got to dwell on what happened the *last* time you hung out. I mean, hugs, lingering physical contact—it drives you *mad*. There is also another former boyfriend that I think about sometimes. He and I had counted eleven places in which we made out in this park downtown. It's so trivial, that number. But I remember it."

"I think we're more prone to keeping sensitivity locked up inside," Christopher surmises of why people still don't fully appreciate the burgeoning big hearts of our young boys today. "After all, being too touchy-feely generally equates to weakness in the male eye, so emotions get covered up. Doesn't mean they're not *there*."

If people were to take the time and really get to know boys, Christopher says, then we'd all see that much of what we interpret as unemotional is really just further evidence of the different ways in which boys choose to express themselves.

"It's more that people are just hard-wired differently," he notes, "and where they invest emotions is just different, hence making it seem as if boys aren't emotional at all, since in comparison, girls invest their emotions in more visible, social situations. But yeah, boys are *very* emotional. Men might even be more emotionally immature than women because they've got all these issues with the emotions they have, and they haven't had as much experience dealing with them in the open like women have. The downside, of course, is that we're all misunderstood."

What would Christopher want people to know about him, if they took the time to get to know him and didn't focus so much on what they thought marked him as so different from everybody else?

"That when you think about it, none of these labels really matter," he tells me in a straightforward tone. "True, I'm gay, I'm deaf, I'm politically conservative, and I'm a vegan. True, I have opinions and beliefs that don't fit a conventional structure, and I'm not embarrassed by it. In the end though, I want companionship and love as surely as anyone else does."

The Rich Kid

I used 2 wake up everyday and wonder if I would survive now I wake up wondering if ill ever feel that way again the only axe u need to wield in destroying our demons is the immense passion 2 help yourself I now love life because I wielded that axe if a once hopeless kid can now thank god 4 the life he has then I shalt not stand alone join me in harmony my brothers I like u can prove that happiness is achievable so go fuckin' get it tigers fight 4 ur happiness because I can tell u that u will find it no questions.

—*Preston Bard, text message*

It's good to be back in high school, especially when it's not your school and you're no longer a teenager. At this high school, a posh private establishment on Manhattan's Upper East Side, a crowd is assembled inside the darkened auditorium on a clear, cold Friday night in February. A quartet of girls, all four of them giddy to see one another, partially blocks my view of the stage. Two of the girls are in black kitten heels and cream-colored tunics cinched at the waist with giant wide belts; the other two wear skinny jeans and off-the-shoulder tops. Everyone in the auditorium is either in jeans or tunics and black leggings. Boys display their baggy, stonewashed denim. The 1980s, evidently, are back.

I'm a sucker for any sort of gathering where there's an aluminum bowl of Doritos and warm six-packs of Coca-Cola Classic standing beside a bowl of melting ice, and this high school rock concert triggers pangs of youthful nostalgia. As a Clash cover band kicks into "Train in Vain," a loner kid in glasses hovers around the snack table glumly helping himself to a fistful of pretzels.

On stage, another student band jump-starts its set with a rousing rendition of "House of the Rising Sun." The kids in the audience sway their hips from side to side while waving their soda-cupped hands slo-mo in the air. It's difficult to make out the lyrics to the next band's opening song, but by its shrieking vocals and the crackling kickback from the audio speakers, I determine they most likely have something to do with sorrow or pain or being misunderstood.

Preston Bard appears downstairs in the school lobby to say a quick hello before darting backstage in time for his band's big performance. His rich dulcet voice belies his eighteen years. He wears a skinny tie, foppish black blazer with thick white pinstripes, and pressed slacks. His hair is a tumbling crest of thick, yellow curls. Between the 1980s retrospect get-up and his well-conditioned locks, I tell him he looks like a cross between Anthony Michael Hall and one of those preppy Whit Stillman characters in *Last Days of Disco*. He immediately gets the reference. (Apart from a few exceptions in the boys I meet along the way, today's teenage boys tend to boast a strong knowledge of retrospective pop culture. We tend to underscore a teen's ability to reference cultural icons and events from decades past.)

"It was the band's idea," says Preston, hiking up his shirt collar. He tells me to enjoy the show and then he's off, barely making it backstage in time for his opening on lead guitar as a reverberating chant of his band's name gets bounced around the auditorium: *"Acid Wash! Acid Wash! Acid Wash!"*

Preston rings me from a ski lift in Aspen. It's December, a few months prior to his rock concert, and he's vacationing there with his family, as he's done his entire life, lodging at a luxury hotel and ski resort—the playground of the rich. He spends the first few days of his vacation with his parents, and then Willow, his girlfriend of three months, joins him. "It's been a trip," says Preston, mountain winds whipping through the wires. "It's been just great. I guess my family's been spoiled with Aspen snow. So our expectation of good skiing is actually extremely high."

That snow-pounded Colorado has declared a state of emergency eludes those gleaning the recreational benefits of its soft, powdery slopes. When Preston first hears about it, he seems genuinely surprised. "I guess in Aspen we're a bunch of spoiled rich folks who don't give a shit," he playfully quips. "We're kind of like, 'What? Oh yeah?'"

Preston tells me that people who don't know him well sometimes use the word "spoiled" to describe him. After all, his dad is a self-made millionaire who founded his own company and charters private jets for business excursions. Preston grew up in the same social circle as the Hilton sisters. "I knew Paris and Nicky before they were actual celebrities," says Preston. "I could tell you all sorts of information about the Hilton family. One thing I will tell you, the family enjoys the publicity. It's just the most fucking disgusting thing. Paris is *not* her image. I've known her since whenever and I can tell you it's basically an act. Basically, everyone thinks the Hiltons have a lot of money but that's actually the most untrue fact of all."

When it comes to facts about money, Preston is frank but cautiously guarded. His girlfriend, he discloses, does not spring from the same ranks of prosperity as his own family, which makes talking about it slightly uncomfortable for him. "I would say she's not on the same economic level as I am at all. But I mean, she has a good, steady life."

For the boys I spoke with whose families were struggling to afford life's basic necessities, there were two categories of teenagers: the Rich Kids and the Poor Kids. The rich kids have everything they want, and the poor kids have . . . *nothing*. For extremely affluent teens like Preston, the divisions are more nuanced, with people divided between the rich and the rich*er.* "To me do I feel very wealthy? Yes, of course," Preston concedes. "But I don't feel quote-unquote *very* wealthy because I don't really exploit what I have. You know, there's always someone higher. I've met people who have so much money and it's just . . . the wealth is just *disgusting.*"

Preston is taking a part in this book with hopes that people—both teenagers and adults—who read about him will come to understand that there's far more to a so-called rich teenage boy than the amount of money in his trust fund.

If all boys have a secret to tell, then for Preston it's hiding a mental disorder that he fought courageously to understand and from which all the currency in the world could not save him—an illness that nearly destroyed his life.

"When someone thinks of a messed up kid they think of the artsy fuck, very dark," posits Preston, whose shiny, well-scrubbed looks don't always jell with society's perception of a kid in crisis. It bothers Preston that sometimes he'll meet people—boys his age included—who presume that just because he doesn't have to worry about money, his life is worry-free. They don't see the real Preston at *all*, he laments. But Preston doesn't want his story to be a sentimental, self-pitying profile about a rich kid with too much money and not enough love who sits around feeling sorry for his misfortune. Rather, per his wishes, this chapter in Preston Bard's life is about a young man in the flush of first love, about longtime suffering and ultimate self-acceptance. Mostly Preston's story is about a mental illness that he prays other boys his age will never have to endure, and the ensuing struggle against that disease, a fight that Preston considers the quintessential defining experience of his adolescent life: "My battle with obsessive-compulsive disorder."

It's early January and Preston has just returned from a few days in Palm Beach where the Bards own a family vacation home—a beachfront *pied-à-terre* with a million-dollar view of the Atlantic. Preston informs me that the trip to Florida was "controversial." He's just finished winter exams and he's already been accepted to his top choice school on the West Coast, a small private college with a prestigious film department and a sleepy suburban locale. But between relaxing rounds on the golf course with his dad and soaking up the Florida sun, there was a night at dinner when, confesses Preston, his voice, *sotto voce*, ascending in volume, "If you gave me a gun it may have been Columbine in that restaurant."

Surrounded by adults—his father, friends of the family—in that restaurant, Preston exuberantly expressed his amorous feelings for Willow, whom Preston credits for completely turning his life around. "I think she may be the one," Preston gushes. "We've both already kind of said 'I do.'"

They met when a slightly buzzed Willow blindly grabbed onto Preston's arm during a Labor Day weekend house party in the Hamptons. Proving, yes, boys are the romantic type, Preston and Willow snuck off from the party, then made out on a rainy, sand-swept beach. He describes the "Lawrence of Arabia sandstorms" swirling in the backdrop, wet sand caking their hair. Since then, it's been mad, mad, *mad* love.

But Preston's adult dinner companions that night in Palm Beach were predictably jaded. "I was vultured by these adults saying it would never happen," Preston angrily

grumbles of talk that he and Willow will never stay together through college (she's heading to school on the East
Coast). "I would have cried if I weren't on SSRIs," he candidly confides. "I called her up and I was like, '*No one* believes in our love, babe.'"

When asked to describe in visceral terms that moment
when said adults threatened to chip away at his romantic
bliss, Preston's voice rises with palpable ire. "What goes
through my head," he furiously recounts, "is *fuck you*.
Why are *you* defining my terms of love? Why can't you
just say, 'you know what? I hope it *does* work out if it
makes you happy.' Why can't people just fucking say that?
I was in a rage. I just got crazy. Willow makes me the happiest man alive. She's my angel. Our love for one another
grows more and more every day. It's the one thing that's
really making me happy in life and my dad won't fucking
pay for a plane ticket for me to visit her. I mean, this is *love*.
Don't fucking tell me it's going to be taken away."

Like a lot of boys his age, Preston has endured enough
pain to appreciate that happiness is not necessarily a basic
human right. Because of his obsessive-compulsive disorder (OCD), Preston has fought tirelessly to eke out joy in
his world, and he is feisty and tenacious in his determination to protect it. He comes alive amid his quest to maintain this happiness at all cost.

"One thing I care about in my life is my happiness,"
he breathlessly declares. "It took me a long time to get
happy and finally I'm there and if you're going to fuck
with that—*man*. I mean, basically I'm a Mafioso putting
a bull's-eye on your head." He pauses, drawing a long,
deep breath. "If you fuck with my happiness," he pointedly declares, "then you're fucking *dead*."

For a long time Preston was miserable. He was a shy
kid at an early age and lacked a steady big brother figure

to pal around with or go to for advice. So in eighth grade, as his family was readying for another holiday in Aspen, his mother tacked up a notice in the Columbia and NYU dorms for a student to act as Preston's paid travel companion on the trip.

"My mom being, you know, very kind of overprotective, just thought it'd be cool to have like some older guy, you know, stay with me and you know, I'd have someone to do stuff with," says Preston of the proposed arrangement. "My mom also wanted help, you know, with the luggage—my mom packs a *shitload.*"

Hart McLaughlin, an undergraduate at New York University, answered the ad. "At first it was obviously a bit awkward," recalls Preston of that first trip to Aspen with Hart. "But towards the end we really started to, you know, take off. I remember one specific moment at the end where, yeah, where we were saying good-bye and I kinda put out my hand for one of those high-five-and-handshake things but I realized halfway through that wasn't appropriate. We gave each other a look and then we hugged." He then quickly adds, laughing a little, "And then the theme music from *Brokeback Mountain* played."

Preston and Hart's blooming friendship quickly became meaningful for both of them. "Preston and I became very close," Hart writes me. "I like to have serious conversations and he has a lot of serious things to say, so maybe that's one reason. But we also find each other immensely entertaining. I don't laugh with anybody as much as I laugh with Preston."

Preston and Hart kept in touch the rest of that year and through the following spring, when Hart joined the Bards once again for an Aspen romp. "Spring vacation was when we really bonded," remembers Preston, who today calls Hart his "best friend" (among several other "best" friends, which I take to be an indicator that Preston forges meaningful connections with many boys). "It was a bit more relaxed. We started to talk about deeper stuff, you know, about girls and just different things."

Their brotherhood bond benefited both young men. As their six-year age gap melted away, Hart and Preston together obsessed over girl problems, watched movies, sketched impromptu comedy skits, and joked around. When Preston was feeling down, Hart could always lift his spirits. "If there was one thing that made our relationship so special," Hart writes, "it was perhaps the fact that even when he was most depressed, he was able to enjoy our conversations, that I was able to remind him of all the things he did love to do. We just talked things through, approached how he was feeling from every angle we could. They were some of the best conversations I've ever had."

By the time Hart accompanied Preston on a three-week family trip to Russia and Turkey, Hart was one of the few friends Preston had who looked beyond his bank account, even if technically Hart was hired help. Their friendship would have flourished regardless of Hart getting paid (outside of the vacations, they spent time hanging out together). "We really looked at each other as friends," says Preston of that vacation during which he and Hart made a sport out of skirt-chasing cute Russian and Turkish girls. "He helped me to be more outgoing over the trip. We really got to know each other quite well."

That summer Hart's presence was especially critical as he consoled Preston throughout the nascent realization that he might have obsessive-compulsive disorder. He hadn't yet been diagnosed, but the more he experienced symptoms of the disease—the badgering thoughts in his head, the constant doorknob touching—and the more self-aware he became that something might be seriously wrong with him, the more Preston relied on Hart. Without Hart by his side during that turbulent time, Preston says that he would have felt completely lost. Preston doesn't know how other boys—those with OCD or any number of other hardships—make it without dependable, long-lasting male friendships in their lives. In a way theirs is a love story, if a platonic one, more *Swingers* or *Stand By Me* than *Brokeback Mountain*. When he couldn't find the words to talk to his parents, when the medical field couldn't prescribe Preston what he needed beyond medication in the way of treating the emotional pain of his OCD, Hart provided what so many boys crave like a tree rooting for water in a desert—a confidant who is always, at any hour, day or night, willing to listen. Declares Preston with a slight catch in his throat: "Hart saved my *life*."

Ninth grade was when Preston's troubles began. "I started to get depressed," recalls Preston of the year when his obsessive-compulsive thoughts and actions began to prevent him from living a normal life. Though he wasn't officially diagnosed until tenth grade, the ever-escalating symptoms of the disorder—the object touching compulsion, the relentless thoughts in his head that would command him to perform certain rituals—gave Preston a sense of being pummeled by a force beyond his control. "The OCD is always there," he tells me, "but freshman year it really skyrocketed."

In the United States, roughly 3.3 million people are afflicted with OCD, with approximately 1 million of that number representing the pediatric population (children between the approximate ages of four and eighteen).[1] Once thought to be a marginally rare disease, OCD currently outranks other mental disorders such as bipolar disorder, panic disorder, and schizophrenia.[2]

"The sampling techniques are never perfect," notes Charles S. Mansueto, director of the Behavior Therapy Center of Greater Washington and member of the Obsessive Compulsive Foundation's scientific advisory board. "We don't have perfect precision when estimating the numbers, nor do we have it with any mental disorder. The data isn't perfectly clear. Some estimates would suggest the rate of OCD occurrence in the United States is as high as 5 or 6 million. In terms of children, that means about one in every hundred school-age kids. And while the precise numbers are interesting, the most important fact is that OCD ranks fourth among common diagnoses of mental illness that people are given, beaten out only by depression, substance abuse, and phobia."[3]

This ravaging anxiety disorder is marked by obsessive compulsions and phobias. People suffering from OCD will often perform rituals such as frequent hand washing, counting, checking, or cleaning in an effort to make these unwanted compulsions or obsessive thoughts disappear. OCD occurs equally in grown men and women, but in adolescence it is diagnosed primarily in boys, where the period of onset is typically reported between the ages of six and fifteen.[4]

"We don't exactly know why boys are diagnosed earlier than girls," explains Mansueto, whose Silver Spring, Maryland–based practice has treated over ten thousand people with OCD and OC spectrum problems such as trichotillomania,[5] body dysmorphic disorder,[6] and Tourette syndrome.[7] "We know that boys are more vulnerable to Tourette syndrome and tic disorders, and these are closely related to OCD. Very often, earlier childhood forms of OCD are often tic-like in manifestation. There are various reasons to speculate about it, but we know that girls' nervous systems and physical makeup are in many ways more resilient and less vulnerable than boys' to different kinds of physical and psychological disruptions in ordinary childhood development."

For Preston, the disruptions have proved untenable. "It is a very rigorous battle determining what is myself and what is the OCD," describes Preston of his daily struggle with the disorder, the symptoms of which can drive Preston to maddening levels of paranoia and despair. "The real lethal aspect of it is that it almost tries to liquidate you. It becomes symbiotic with your personality and who you are. With me it's like, 'Is this the OCD thinking this or is it *me* thinking this?'"

As far back as fourth grade, Preston was hearing voices inside his head that drove him to desperation. He thought he was going crazy. "This voice in my head would say, 'You're *gonna* die,'" he solemnly recalls, "and then another voice would say, 'You're *gonna* catch a horrible, deadly disease.'"

Soon Preston began seeing a psychotherapist. But he was scared to reveal too much in case the therapist thought that he was "crazy." "I hid it well," says Preston. "I thought, 'What the fuck *was* this thing?' But I hid it well. I wasn't very open with my emotions because I thought that if I told her I had a voice in my head she'd send me to a psychiatric ward."

Mansueto plies the psychiatric term "egodystonic," a type of behavior that is inconsistent with one's fundamental beliefs, in describing the "voice" to which Preston refers. "People [with OCD] often talk about a 'voice' that told them something," explains Mansueto. "It's a way of describing the fact that some of their thoughts seem quite alien. The difference between true psychosis and OCD, and how we make a differential diagnosis between them, is that in OCD, the patients will understand that their ideas come out of their own imagination, that they are not inserted there from without by another entity, that they are generated from their own mechanism even though they don't want them to be there."

One of the great challenges facing patients with OCD, according to Mansueto, is to learn that the voices they hear in their heads are actually part of their own thought process and that through the right kind of therapy and medication they can find the power to control them. But this is often a long-standing and exceptionally difficult process requiring a properly therapeutic doctor-patient relationship.

Preston's three years in therapy with this particular psychotherapist started in fifth grade (they terminated their relationship when Preston was in eighth grade because Preston didn't think that she was helping him). Preston revealed enough that he believes the doctor should have at least *suspected* that he had OCD. "I don't know how the fuck she didn't pick up on the fact that I had OCD," he says now, "because I had told her a little bit about the voices. She said it was anxiety. No shit, it's anxiety. Anyone who's going to have a fuckin' voice in their head is going to be *anxious*." Preston huffs when recounting his frustrating efforts to deal with his OCD and the accompanying difficulties that he's encountered in professional help along the way.

Things grew infinitely worse when, toward the end of eighth grade, Preston came across an article in the *New York Post* about a thirteen-year-old boy who died of cancer. The article featured before and after pictures of the boy as his cancer metastasized. The images panicked Preston beyond belief. "The 'after' picture just stuck with me, it was almost like a demon and it made me develop a fear of getting cancer," he says. Indeed, disease phobia is typical among those dealing with OCD. "My biggest fear has always been getting a disease. Especially cancer. I can't watch St. Jude's commercials with kids that have gone through chemotherapy. That summer I actually had to leave camp early because I had this voice in my head constantly telling me I'm going to have cancer. Or, if I stepped on the sidewalk this way or that way then bad things are going to happen to my family."

The voices pursued Preston with dogged persistence, who was still unaware of what was happening to him. "At the time it was more physical compulsions," Preston details of the mind games that his brain would play on him, voices demanding that he perform various physical acts: "Touch *this*, what will happen? Touch *that*, what will happen?" The compulsions became, in his words, "almost idolatrous," beckoning Preston to succumb to them in a disturbing Svengali-like manner. Preston found himself surrendering to these unmitigated urges with the fanaticism of a zealot.

Then, almost miraculously, between the summer of eighth and ninth grades, Preston was able to "kill it," or "massively suppress" the voices in his head. To his immeasurable relief, the paranoia that he'd get cancer and the unmitigated urges to touch things ceased.

"What happened was I said, okay, *this* is what I have to do," he recalls of the scheme he devised on his own to exorcise the compulsions. "Since I had to touch the towel seven times, I had to now touch it six times. And then five, four, three, two, one . . . until I was able to literally delete my compulsions."

Preston's remission lasted about five months.

In ninth grade Preston's OCD returned with a vengeance. It caused him to feel like a recluse who didn't belong. Even though he had a solid group of devoted school friends, plus Hart, his burgeoning OCD made him feel like a social pariah. So far as Preston was concerned, at this point in his life he was alone.

"I began to get depressed," he winces of that dusky period, "and it was because I was insecure. Now, we're *all* insecure. I was shy, you know, I was shy with girls, but I wasn't exactly really *shy* now that I look back on it. It was almost like the OCD *made* me shy. I was so obsessed with my insecurity that I just felt like that's what got me depressed. It was really the OCD that drove me insane. And this is where the OCD just gets *really* weird."

Around ninth grade, Preston reveals that the OCD made him think he was gay. This was not about sexual longing, he says, or any cultural taboos where his friendship with Hart was concerned. Preston did not desire sexual relationships with men (if he *had* the situation might have been easier to deal with, he admits). But whenever he passed a man on the street a voice inside his head would demand that he hold his breath. The voice dictated that if Preston didn't hold his breath, if he took a deep breath in, than he would be literally inhaling that man, consuming him in a sexual manner. It was a confusing and frightening time.

"I don't know what the fuck was going on with me," recalls Preston of the tormented period that consumed most of ninth grade. Like many other boys exhibiting symptoms of OCD who don't yet know they *have* it, Preston could make no sense of these bizarre, uncontrollable impulses: "To me I just think that I'm this weird, *fucked up* kid."

Per Mansueto, who has treated teens with similar symptoms, Preston's fears and anxieties are actually quite common, even among adolescents without OCD. "Concerns about sexual possibilities are very typical of teenagers who are still figuring out their identities," states Mansueto.

"Most teenagers have a normal developmental concern or fear about their sexuality and most people at that age want to be heterosexual for a variety of cultural, religious, and sociological reasons. But kids with OCD often have a vivid imagination. They have strong emotional systems and are constantly stirred by thought. And this causes them great distress. They think that because these thoughts are intrusive that they must be true. They feel so threatened by these normal fears that they come up with their own solution, such as holding their breath. As the ritual becomes more and more comfortable they keep doing it. They avoid and escape the things that arouse their particular fears. And unfortunately, relying on these escape rituals actually locks in their fear, pushing them right back in consciousness."

Meanwhile, Preston's parents didn't know about any of this. Other than his going through a "depression," they had no idea to what extent Preston was suffering. At this point, he had yet to tell them about the menacing voices in his head or such confusing impulses as having to touch a light switch seventeen times. He's always had a strained relationship with his mother (whom Preston refers to as an "emotional powder keg who has an intolerance of personal flaws"), and he wasn't quite sure what to say to his father when he was dealing with these uncomfortable feelings. Many boys in Preston's position would have felt equally vulnerable, and afraid that nobody would believe them—or worse, that they *would*.

How do you tell a parent that you're scared because the voice in your head is making you hold your breath every time a man passes you on the street?

In the spring of ninth grade, Preston's struggle with OCD led him to become suicidal. "I hit ground zero," Preston remembers of that day he came home from Palm Beach and, crossing the George Washington Bridge, heard a voice that commanded him to jump over it. He was seized by terror, deep and bottomless. "I didn't want to *die*," he shakily clarifies in retrospect. "I wanted the suffering to *end*."

According to a study conducted at Duke University, boys between the ages of fifteen and nineteen are four times more likely to commit suicide than girls (although girls are more likely to attempt the act).[8] Two of Preston's friends have tried to kill themselves; both attempts, drug and alcohol related, and his OCD almost drove him, too, over the brink. "Boys are more likely to do themselves in when they are in crisis because they choose more irreversibly lethal means," explains Ethan Pollack. "In suicide one of the factors you have to look at is how reversible the attempt is. Women use pills, they cut their wrists—those are highly reversible methods. Jumping off something, driving an automobile when you're under the influence—those are generally *not* reversible."

Ultimately a psychiatrist Preston met during a two-week stint at an all-boys boarding school in New Hampshire in tenth grade correctly diagnosed his OCD and guided Preston through his immediate crisis. He essentially laid down the law. "If you don't tell your parents [about the suicidal feelings] right away," the psychiatrist explained, "I legally have to."

But was Preston ready to tell his parents, and were they ready to listen? Like a lot of teenage boys, Preston was resentful of his parents "always" thinking they knew the answer. He feared that if he told his parents the truth, they'd be ill-prepared to deal with it in a manner that was emotionally healthy for him. He worried that they wouldn't believe him, or somehow condemn him as though it were his fault. Given everything he was going through, Preston was in no mood for his parents to dismiss his problems as "exaggerated" as they had done so in the past.

"The only reason I had not told my parents is because in the past every time I came to my mom with a problem she always thought she knew the fucking answer," Preston says. "So when I said, 'I'm having headaches due to OCD,' she said 'Oh, it's because of this,' 'Oh, it's because of that.' And I was like, 'No, it's because of something *else*. When you have an OCD moment the brain is experiencing a moment of stress. No one wants their whole fucking life to be a headache.' And then she would always say, 'No,' and she'd actually get fucking mad at me for coming to her with a problem. It taught me to not come to her with anything."

Majy Gibboney, an educator in the Los Angeles public school system, has noticed the same resistance among teenage boys in her own high school classes in disclosing troubling secrets to their parents. Teens felt that talking to their parents was moot, because they often leaped to conclusions that weren't necessarily true. "Boys do not need to be told the 'shoulds' of life," Gibboney proffers during our conversation. "Rather, they need to be questioned *calmly*. We need to share our observations and let *them* figure it out and tell *us* what's wrong. Too many adults assume that boys have sifted through it all and have the answers neatly filed away articulately in their brain. *No.* The solutions are scattered all over the place. Adults *don't* always know what the problem is. And believe me, boys *hate it* when you guess wrong."[9]

After carefully discussing such concerns with his psychiatrist, Preston chose an upcoming weekend in Palm Beach to finally talk to his parents. Hart accompanied him on the trip. (He was no longer getting paid but traveling as Preston's guest and good friend.) Terrified of what everyone might think of him, Preston spilled his guts to Hart first. "He is there for me *every* second I need him," recalls Preston of Hart's compassionate response. "He was my rock. He was my therapist, best friend—everything all in one. Every time I was with him we'd always be talking about my problems. He sat and listened, he held me through it. He is there for me *every* second I need him. He said, 'Dude, I'm here for you *all* the time. Parents—it's just different when they're your parents. That's the way it works.'"

Without Hart by his side, Preston might never have mustered up the courage to break down to his parents and disclose everything he had been going through. "I ended up crying it out," he says, which proved to be a tremendous relief. "My dad was very calm with it. That's why I love my dad so much." His mother, Preston tells me, was also supportive, if more visibly unnerved by Preston's shocking confession. "My mom was very surprised," he remembers of that watershed moment. "But she was there for me."

But even parents with the best intentions can't be *all* things to their children. We can't be the parent that establishes curfew rules *and* the best friend with whom our kids talk about masturbating to the cute girl at school or what it feels like to get a blowjob for the first time or being a reluctant virgin at eighteen years old. And boys have a right to talk about these things with someone who isn't going to chastise or malign them for their feelings.

Boys need other boys (or girls, in some cases) to talk with, to listen to their problems. They need at least one person in whom they are consistently able to confide. To keep boys grounded and sane, it's crucial that we encourage our young people to forge trusting, enduring friendships with others, to show them that boys can be close friends without all the unhealthy and unnecessary assumptions about their sexuality. With Preston and Hart as an example, such tight-knit and reliable friendships between teenagers can be a key building block in helping boys form better relationships with their parents.

It is Hart whom Preston thanks for drawing him out of the darkness and helping him to form a more meaningful relationship with his mother and father. Without Hart, Preston tells me, there were days when his anxiety and depression got so bad that he might not have salvaged any will to get out of bed. Says Preston, "Hart ended up almost giving up his life for me."

Now in twelfth grade, Preston says his suicidal tendencies have subsided, though they have not completely disappeared. He's still being treated long distance by the New Hampshire–based shrink he first met in boarding school (they correspond via telephone and web cam) and takes four doctor-prescribed medications. Prozac, Luvox, and Xanax, along with weekly talk therapy, mitigate the recurring symptoms of Preston's OCD.[10] Cialis offsets the sexual side affects of his OCD medication.[11] "Now when I get a suicidal thought it's a lot less powerful," says Preston. "It's just something along the lines of, 'okay, this sucks, it's giving me an anxiety attack. How do I get rid of it?'"

Preston knows that his OCD can never be cured completely, that he'll be wrestling with its symptoms for a long time to come. He'll mostly likely spend the rest of his life taking prescribed medications, and that too is a burden. Sometimes the medication has to be tweaked, the dosage adjusted. The treatment for obsessive-compulsive disorder requires constant maintenance. But Preston does not have a single regret. If he could magically become that boy who never had OCD, if he could erase it from his brain, annihilating it retroactively like a character in *Eternal Sunshine of the Spotless Mind*, he says he wouldn't. Because if he did, it would mean obliterating all the other parts of himself that he's grown to admire and love.

"All the tragedy I've faced," Preston declares with un-flinching conviction, "has made me the person I am."

Preston's Manhattan penthouse takes up an entire floor, with spectacular views of the city. It's the night after his big concert and Preston, tousled bed-head and barefoot in a pair of frayed jeans, stands outside the doors of the private apartment elevator.

After I commit a grave misstep in mistaking the lead guitar for the bass ("I'm really surprised you don't know this," Preston snaps), I marginally win back his respect by complimenting the collection of boyhood relics assembled in his bedroom: a Cookie Monster stuffed animal, sports paraphernalia, an Elmo doll.

"There was a period a while ago when I wasn't so happy and I wanted to find stuff to make me happy and I wanted to redecorate it," Preston explains, sitting down at his desk. "I never got around to doing that because I kind of stopped caring. I was like, whatever, this is my room. I don't have to take the time to make my room look trendy. It is what it is."

There's a web cam on Preston's computer through which he and his psychiatrist conduct their long-distance therapy sessions. "My shrink and I have actually thought about patenting it," says Preston of their high-tech communication system. Where his other doctors "just kinda sucked," this one has proven to be a real hero. "He's helped me differentiate between the way I feel about certain things and certain behaviors and my OCD: *This* is OCD, and *this* is you."

Stacked neatly in Preston's bookshelf are biographies of male celebrities such as Johnny Depp and Daniel Day-

Lewis, role models Preston idolized when he was fifteen and sixteen and in the thick of his depression. "They were all pretty unpopular in high school, you know," he explains of seeking solidarity among these alleged loners-turned-movie stars. "I started viewing myself as a tortured artist and I looked up to quote-unquote other tortured artists like David Lynch, Quentin Tarantino, Robin Williams, and Tom Cruise."

That he considers Tom Cruise a "tortured artist" could be the most curious discovery of my fact-finding mission on the secret lives of boys. I can do nothing to mask my visible disappointment.

"Reading his biography, his dyslexia, his father fucked him *up*," Preston immediately counters. "Okay, so I wouldn't say Cruise is in the same league as Quentin Tarantino. He's my favorite director—I aspire to be like him. He said that *True Romance* is about how he just could not find a woman who liked him for who he was. And I *really* relate to that."

When it comes to women, if there's one fixture in Preston's room of which he's most proud, it's a framed photograph of himself and Willow skiing in Aspen, huddled together on a snow-capped slope, the wintry Colorado sun glistening against their perfect hair. The happy holiday snapshot symbolizes the love he and Willow share, as well as how far Preston has journeyed since junior high, when not having a girlfriend was a main trigger of his depression. Until he met Willow, his sense of failure was mostly based on not getting laid.

"I almost put too much dependence on it," Preston admits of his obsession with finding a girlfriend. Unlike the boys I met who seemed comfortable with their virginity, Preston's was a burden that, he now views in retrospect, was a result of his OCD making him obsess over it. "I was just never like 'Okay, so I'm a guy who doesn't hook up with a lot of girls, big deal.' I almost looked down on myself for not hooking up with a lot of girls and that was just bad. That really lowered my self-esteem. 'Cuz I blamed it on myself. I was asking 'What am *I* doing wrong?' Instead of 'What can I *do* to just make my life happy?'"

But no matter how many people told him otherwise, Preston couldn't shake his shame-based insecurity. "I would have taken a girlfriend over *anything*," he tells me. "It was a big part of my loneliness. I never really found a guy like me to relate to in this particular love situation. A lot of my friends either had girlfriends or got a lot of ass and no one could really understand what I felt and sympathize with that. So, I had no proof. It was just a big, sad part of my life. That's why Willow and I have such a good relationship. I'm really thankful for her in my life."

Willow came around at a particularly tempestuous period in Preston's adolescence. Although at this point he was being treated for his OCD, the medications prescribed for the disease lose their efficacy over time and occasionally need to be tweaked. When this happens, the symptoms of OCD often temporarily resurge. (For this reason, Mansueto suggests for OCD patients a complementary behavioral treatment tool known as ERP, or exposure and response prevention, that guides the patient through gradual and methodical means to confront the themes of his obsessions that provoke his anxiety.) "I was going through a lot of shit with my OCD, the worst that I'd ever gone through," Preston recalls. "It was a bad period of six months, but it felt like six *years*."

Following that first cinematic romp in the sand and a few flirtatious follow-up text messages ("I had a really good time w/ u. Hope 2 C U again soon") Preston realized, "Okay, I think she's pretty into me." But he still wasn't sure whether or not to push forward. "I'd been going through this OCD thing, so I didn't know *what* I wanted."

Then he and Willow ran into each other at a dinner party.

"Overrated," Preston deadpans of his first sexual experience. "By every single standard. After it was done I was like, I spent the ages from twelve 'til now like worrying about this shit? What the *fuck*? Now it's amazing but then it was just like, 'Oh my God, I can't *believe* I wasted all that time obsessing about it.'"

Although teenage sex is often a humiliating proposition, for Preston there are added complications caused by the Cialis. He wasn't sure how Willow would react to the notion of Preston popping a pill between required school community service projects and study circles in order to ensure that when he and Willow were together he'd get a hard-on.

"I basically said, 'I want to be honest with you,'" recalls Preston of what he dreaded would be the most awkward precoital conversation in teenage conjugal history. "'If we're going to be having sex, I need to tell you that I actually need to take a pill in order to have sex.' I was expecting that she'd be weirded out by it, so I asked her, 'Do you care?' She goes, 'No.' At that moment I was like, 'Okay, this girl is the one for me.' It was really the defining factor for our relationship because I honestly don't know a lot of teenage girls who would be willing to do that. I thought that's *really* liking someone."

And so, despite the 1,500 or so miles that will separate them come fall, Preston has no qualms about making their long-distance love affair last. "Ninety-nine percent of the reason that people break up in college is that one of the partners in the couple wants to branch out," Preston points out. "I know I don't need that. What Willow's offered me I'm not sure if a lot of people—and I'm not talking about teenagers—if *anyone* could. When I call up Willow, because I have OCD attacks, when I say, 'Babe, I'm having a suicidal-provoking OCD attack,' she says, 'Do you want me to come over?' I mean, people have broken up because one of the people in the relationship has a disease like OCD. The OCD has made me try to believe that I shouldn't be going out with Willow anymore, that I don't like her. I have told Willow this. We're still together. I don't need anything *else*."

"Personally, I don't think I'm like a lot of other rich kids," Preston pronounces as we stroll past upscale baby clothing boutiques, a candy-colored shop filled with preppy striped belts and polo shirts, a pet store filled with designer dog duds, and a veritable motorcade of Lincoln Signatures parked alongside the curb. "The essential socialite horse and carriage," quips Preston, whose family employs private drivers, many of whom have acted as Preston's *de facto* therapists during winding drives through Central Park. Preston emits a subtle, self-deprecating scoff. "When everyone imagines the rich, people assume that it's paradise," he says. "People assume it's *everything*."

We lunch at a crowded Italian bistro where Preston and the *maître d'* embrace in warm familial fashion. Over the house specialty pasta and iced teas with blood oranges halved on the glass, we talk about movies, about what kind of experience he hopes college will be for him, and about Willow. He winds pasta around his fork while waxing romantic on the possibility of their life together—marriage, kids, a house. A few times during our meal, Preston politely excuses himself from the table to wave hello and have a short chat with fellow restaurant regulars. The atmosphere is bright and convivial, like nothing can touch the shafts of soft winter sunlight that pour in through the restaurant windows and land on the fur-coated women lunching at the table next to us, their fat diamond rings glinting aggressively in the light.

"You know, some people say that depression is a disease of the affluent," Preston remarks of the scene. "It's true. We're economically advantaged. But emotionally we're *not* advantaged. Because if we don't have to worry about putting a meal on our plate then our mind is going to allow us to worry about other things."

A moment later, sadness falls over Preston's face. He stares up from his plate, thoughtfully sets down his fork, and bluntly declares, as though realizing that the lie he's just told can't possibly be true, no matter how desperately he wants to believe it: "OCD is a *demon*."

Later that night, Hart sends me an email. When all is said and done, he probably knows Preston better than anyone, maybe even his parents. His comforting words continue to rescue Preston from the consuming guilt that his problems are a result of his being advantaged in a way that most teenagers are not, that his OCD is a punishment for being rich.

"Preston went through a hell of a lot," writes Hart. "He is still going through a hell of a lot, perhaps always *will* be going through a hell of a lot. His wealth, as I think it should be clear enough already, spared him none of it. And never *will*."

The Average American Kid

> Since 9/11, I guess it's just a battle against radicalism, so the modern Muslim kids who are basically just average Americans don't make the news. I guess the radical ones are the only ones who make the news. There are not that many Muslims in America, so what they take is all they see in the news so when they see a beheading that's what they think of when they think of a Muslim. If I were a Christian I don't know what I'd feel. I guess we deserve it because of those guys. But I don't feel, like, shame—shame would have something to do with being guilty.
>
> —*Aziz Mohammad*

High school bowling is *far* more competitive than I thought.

"When you walk into the alley on a match day there are like three hundred or four hundred families there to watch," says Indiana native Aziz Mohammad of the hometown buzz on bowling. The small Indianapolis suburb where he lives is *so* tiny, Aziz estimates that its radius measures two miles. "I don't even think it's on the map," he quips of why bowling may just be the most exciting thing to hit the place since WiFi Internet.

Like any seriously committed bowler, Aziz owns his own bowling ball and matching bag. At team practice, he wears a collared bowling shirt with his name sewn in sweeping calligraphy on its front left pocket, and a pair of worn-in bowling shoes. Owning your own shoes, Aziz observes, makes perfect economic sense given the price of rentals at most bowling alleys. He's stumped that more people don't make the investment. After all, he notes with derisive pride, bowling is one of America's top-ranked participant sports.

"It's *huge*," Aziz says, gently mocking the crowd of spectators that gathers at the local Indianapolis suburban lanes for his high school bowling team's weekly matches. "It's like a junior high soccer game at some other school. There's even indoor picnicking." He laughs as he provides colorful visuals of packed lunches and soda pop on the sidelines, parents and supporters cheering and doing the wave like it's the Super Bowl. Then he suddenly clears his throat. "Bowling seems easy," he tells me in an unabashedly earnest tone, "but it's actually really *difficult*."

Aziz and his teammates learned the hard way that, as vulnerable as bowling is to cheeky ridicule—the Big Lebowski is not exactly Tom Brady—it's a demanding sport that requires inexhaustible physical stamina and mental focus. "The funny thing is we won our first game," he says of his high school bowling team's freshman effort. "We went out and celebrated. See, at the beginning you don't know who's good yet. The first team we played was so bad so we thought everybody was like that. They had it all over the school intercom. We were like 'Yeah, we're so good, we beat them by a landslide!'"

However, the next week, Aziz's team was destroyed 30 to 0, its high-spirited momentum dashed like a twelve-pound house ball blasted down the gutter. "After that, it was basically a fight for who's not last," Aziz glumly recalls of a follow-up string of humiliating defeats. "We only came close to winning again once, when we played that first team again and lost by only two points. Our final record was one and twelve. Nobody ever heard us on the school intercom announcements for the rest of the season."

While the 2006–2007 bowling team at Aziz's private, all-boys Catholic high school failed to live up to its initial promise of kingpin victory, seventeen-year-old Aziz has never let it get him down. He's a roll-with-the-punches kind of kid, good-naturedly poking fun at himself and not taking life too seriously. "It was the first year we had it," he shrugs of his amateurish bowling squad. "Compared to these other teams we didn't have a *chance*. The big-time Division 1 teams actually had practice every single day. At one school they actually cut the majority of kids who try out. That team only has seven kids on the team. One kid on it bowled a 310. I was struggling to get a 180."

Despite the team's losing record, jovial members celebrated at an end-of-season banquet where they received their varsity letters and jackets. "I didn't get a jacket," Aziz gently guffaws, refusing to pretend that a mediocre average on a second-tier bowling squad marks him as a high school stud. "People will rip on you at school," he confesses with steady self-assuredness, "but it's all in good nature. I mean, even the word 'bowling' is pretty bad. It's something you can say you like to do but, you know, to most people at school, it's not something to be *proud* of. I mean that's, like, getting a jacket that says 'Chess' or 'Backgammon' on it."

When I set out to write a book about boys, many parents urged me to include a chapter about an "average kid." The term was not intended as an insult. Average doesn't imply that a boy lacks personality or isn't intelligent or is boring. Well, perhaps the average boy is a *little* boring compared to some of the other types, but only because he doesn't get into trouble. According to the parents I spoke with, the average boy doesn't inspire the same electric buzz as some of the more high-profile types who generate newspaper headlines for their drug use or clinical depression or penchant for rebellious behavior at school. On the contrary, they noted, the average teenage boy is reasonably happy, earns consistently decent grades, makes curfew every night. The average boy rarely, if ever, gives parents any considerable grief. He can be depended on for baby-sitting younger siblings, taking in the mail, doing the occasional grocery shopping. The average boy is well admired by those who know him and is friends with pretty much everybody. He never causes a ripple at school, is never picked on, never initiates scuffles. He is quiet but not a loner, smart but not in an extraordinary way. The average kid turns in his homework and teachers generally like his easygoing nature. He is polite and well disciplined, the sort of boy who keeps his hair neatly trimmed in the back. But because he is so well behaved, lament the parents of such teens, the average kid rarely stands out. He risks getting lost in the shuffle of all the other boys at school who were either awarded Best In Everything or, on the opposite end of the spectrum, turned up in local news reports and at the principal's office and were in constant crisis, crisis, *crisis*.

Aziz Mohammad, a practicing Muslim whose parents were born in Syria, is one of these average American teenage boys. He's a regular middle-class kid with an admittedly lackluster bowling average and the same typical concerns as any other high school senior—college, prom, parties. His parents are both successful doctors. He listens to pop and rock music, goes to the movies, watches popular TV shows. He fights with his brothers and sisters. His religious views are "moderate." Per Islamic law, he prays on his own five times every day, and on Fridays, if Aziz doesn't have school, he'll head to the local mosque. He fasts during Ramadan. But he's a "normal kid," he contends, "a modern Muslim—your typical average American teen."

"Aziz is a living example of what an American youth can be," comments an employee of the Youth Programming and Services Department, Islamic Society of North

America (ISNA) who knows Aziz personally. "He lives his religion not only through his spiritual practices, but also through his academic accomplishments, involvement in sports activities, and continuous contribution and involvement in the development of the well-being of the American society. He is an example of how the Islamic faith can inspire American youth not only to refrain from violence, drugs, and other challenges facing them, but also to reach their potential as leaders in their society and as agents of positive change in this world."

Above all, Aziz's happy-go-lucky, socially well-rounded, average-guy image negates the lingering stereotype that many people still envision when it comes to Muslim teens in a post-September 11 America.

"I guess I'll be your first," Aziz announces during our initial conversation, debunking the notion that all teenage boys are lonely or depressed or weird. "I actually feel well liked. I don't want to be immodest and say I'm the most *popular* kid at school, but I don't think I feel isolated much. Because, generally, the way it works is that half the kids take tough classes and the other half don't. The strictly honors and AP classes—those are the kids I'm with. It helps to just constantly be around people and be constantly doing stuff. The more time you spend by *yourself* the more lonely you *are*."

Because of his cultural background Aziz risked sticking out at his private Catholic high school with its predominantly white, Catholic student body (his parents chose to enroll him there because, academically, it's one of the best schools around). But he made a conscious decision *not* to let that happen. There are boys described in this book who refuse to be social in the ways generally expected of teenagers—parties, study groups, school dances—boys who reject any notion of high school homogeneity and resist any attempts to become one with the in-crowd, so to speak. Aziz is not one of them. While he has never surrendered his personal identity at school, he has acquiesced to the status quo, maintaining an open mind about ways in which to participate in school activities, enthusiastically journeying down different extracurricular paths—bowling and varsity track, for example—in order to become an assimilated member of his high school student body on both the social and academic levels.

"Maybe freshman year when I first went to Catholic school, when I prayed before class and I sort of sat in the corner I felt isolated," Aziz remembers of his first few solitary days in high school. "But as time goes by you get used to it and you blend in."

To blend or not to blend: This is the litmus test by which one might differentiate the so-called average boy from the more classic individualist, say, of the sort inspired by the James Dean prototype. Aziz doesn't yield to dominant cultural zeitgeist at school out of lack of self-esteem or personal weakness—it's clear that Aziz adheres to a strong personal code of moral and cultural ethics—but he also doesn't possess any commanding impetus to alienate himself from popular conventional culture the way other teens sometimes do to prove their individuality.

The average boy doesn't *need* to be different.

Boys who want to succeed socially at school, offers Aziz, must learn to make certain concessions in the way they view their place in the world. Boys can't be closed off and oppositional and expect people at school to like them. Per Aziz, it's cool to be yourself, but you've got to mesh a little with the mainstream. In other words, it helps to be a little on the average side.

"It's multifactorial," Aziz posits of his winning efforts to forge connections with the in-crowd at school.

Aziz's attitude represents the thrust of the young male/American melting pot philosophy: While proud of his Muslim faith, religion is not the single defining factor in life. "If you don't hold stuff in all the time then people don't look at you like a weirdo," states Aziz. "You sort of have to dress like everybody—you sort of have to blend in. I mean, you can dress your own way but don't, like, show up to school in a turban. It's just the way it is. Everybody has misconceptions about everyone. If you want to avoid the stereotyping, you have to mesh as much as you can, but without losing your entire identity. This goes for everyone, regardless of religion. It's a delicate balance. Also, if you want to be social, don't go home at 2:30 after school. Join a club. Join a sports team. The key is to get *involved*."

The Crusaders for Life club meets weekly after school. Members of the pro-life group posse discuss such issues as abortion, stem cell research, and euthanasia—all the "hot topics." They attend the occasional protest rally. The group marched on Washington, D.C., but Aziz chose not to participate. "It's not like a club that requires, like, *crazy* dedication," he explains. He joined the group his sophomore year, and while he does not consider himself a radical pro-lifer by any stretch, he has developed a keen intellectual and scientific interest in right-to-life issues as influenced by the Catholic curriculum at school. "After the whole Dr. Kevorkian thing in the '90s I was like '*Whoa*,'" he remembers. "It really stuck with me. And then all the stuff we learned about in health class. They had this one story about a girl who gave birth by herself in a bathroom at prom and then threw the baby out and then went back out into prom. I started learning about partial-birth abortions and we talked about it in theology class how Catholics believe when it's a piece of tissue versus a living thing. That all got me interested."

Aziz isn't certain whether his parents have any particular reservations about his joining a Catholic right-to-life club (since they send him to a Catholic school, he assumes they'd be fine with it, even if the group's primary pro-life mission presents various conflicting viewpoints between the Islamic and Catholic stances on right-to-life issues). "I don't even know if they know I'm in it," Aziz acknowledges, as though the thought has just occurred to him. "It's not like I e-mail my parents every day and tell them what I *do* every day."

But Aziz does keep his parents abreast of most goings-on in his life, if inadvertently, because none of the goings-on are reckless or controversial or juicy enough to be kept secret in his opinion.

On the dating front, for example, Aziz doesn't have a girlfriend, equally a reflection of his conservative upbringing and a lack of strong personal desire to date any one girl in particular. Why be tied down during such a capricious period as adolescence? With college just around the corner, this reasoning resonates with many boys today. Some boys I spoke with made the choice to date girls casually while others chose to postpone any pairing off until such time as they were ready for a "serious relationship." (And some, of course, despite their best efforts, were just not getting *laid*.) "My parents are somewhat against it," Aziz reveals of any hypothetical romantic entanglements that might roll along. "They wouldn't be happy with that. They think it'll be distracting. It's like, 'Keep your mind on school. It's not like you're gong to *marry* her.' But yeah, I also don't have the time. It's a matter of choice."

In accordance with his Muslim beliefs, Aziz also abstains from alcoholic beverages. Even on a recent family excursion to Cancun when Aziz and some friends were free to run wild while their parents were busy with a medical conference back at the hotel, Aziz did not sneak a single *cerveza*. "Mostly it's a religious thing," he discloses. "But it makes a lot of sense. The wisdom behind it is that [Islam] says theoretically you can drink in moderation but since a lot of people don't know when to stop, they say just stay away from it."

Aziz confides that his non-Muslim friends at school do not make him feel self-conscious about his decision, mostly because he doesn't make a big deal out of it. His logic is that going to a party but not drinking generally doesn't raise as many eyebrows as staying at home by yourself on a Saturday night watching TV. Teens are pretty receptive to cultural differences among boys, he believes, so long as boys are upfront about them and express conviction about their personal choices. "People usually drink for themselves," he assertively points out, "not for others. When I'm with kids who drink they don't care that I'm not drinking. They want to get wasted, not me. Besides, from what I hear it tastes pretty bad."

At school and around town, Aziz hasn't encountered much in the way of discrimination. And while Islam has been pushed into the international spotlight over the past several years, and Muslim Americans have experienced intense discrimination, Aziz doesn't waste much time pondering the public perception of the Muslim community. He argues that most of the time Muslims are suspect unnecessarily, their normal, everyday behavior hyperbolically scrutinized as a potential threat. He knows that CNN spots showcasing acts of violence committed by radical Islamic fundamentalists do not apply to him. He knows that family vacations to Syria to visit relatives (most of whom live in Damascus) are the same as many other sun-filled family holidays. They focus on bonding with cousins, relaxing, and taking weekend trips to a beachfront resort hotel for dips in the azure-blue Mediterranean.

Like any other high school senior hoping to get into a good college, Aziz spends most of first semester bogged down in homework assignments for his AP English class. He's already been assigned a weighty reading list of some forty books. "It's usually standard to read forty to sixty pages a night," he grumbles of the semester's hefty work load. "The teacher has to have a way to make sure we're reading so there's either a written or oral test in class. It's like Socratic method where he'll just call on people, which gets mildly annoying because nobody feels like reading *all* those books."

Aziz had hoped to coast through his senior year, but after getting deferred from his top choice school (to which he applied early decision), first semester grades unfortunately *do* count. "I actually had to study a *lot* this year," begrudges Aziz, who has applications pending at University of Michigan, Yale, Northwestern, Johns Hopkins, and the University of Pennsylvania.

Aziz and I talk about whether being a cultural minority gives prospective students any sort of edge in the cutthroat universe of college admissions. Will his being Muslim help him to secure a freshman spot at an Ivy League school? "Yeah," he warily murmurs, "but I'm also under the Catholic umbrella because of my school. I mean, I don't know, colleges say that they don't care, that they don't try to accept minorities. I actually don't even remember anywhere on the application asking for my religion."

When fighting for those inch-thick envelopes in the mail come admissions time in April and May, most teens have no choice but to rely on their grades, a stack of extracurricular activities, and luck. (The competition getting into top-ranked colleges is stiff; many highly intelligent boys, like Apollo, the Indie Fuck, faced crushing rejections from first choice schools.) Aziz doesn't rank among the top few students in his graduating class, but he pulls down a solid GPA of A's and B's. He works hard for his grades. "Last year I used to get stressed out and this year I have *twice* as much work," he heavily sighs. "I used to get overwhelmed the night before a test. I used to have to pick *what* test to study for. I don't know if teachers conspired against us or what the deal was, but this year I just stopped. Maybe it's because it's senior year. I still do everything I'm assigned, but I tried to stop caring about it so much. If I listen in class I'm usually fine. But I *do* have to do the work to do well."

Math and biology are his strong subjects. Aziz also cites evolutionary genetics as one of his main academic interests. "It's pretty cool stuff," he says, "learning about our origins, studying three-to five-foot-tall humans running away from predators like these big cats and hyenas. I like Punit squares too, and studying certain traits—recessive or dominant—and seeing how the offspring will come out in probability."

While Aziz hasn't settled on a definite career path, he's considering tracks in both medicine and business. He plans on spending the summer volunteering three days a week at a local hospital in Indianapolis and taking a part-time job at Best Buy to earn some sales experience should he pursue a graduate program in business management. His parents have yet to persuade him in either direction. "I'm really open to anything," he cheerily announces, "because there's this huge, I don't know, misconception around here that you have to be a doctor or else you won't make money in anything else. But I mean, it's not *what* you do but *how* you do it."

In May, after fielding rejections from several colleges, Aziz puts a deposit down at the University of Michigan.

"I mean, all the other schools were kind of *reach* schools," he shrugs when he receives the leafy-thin rejection letters throughout the spring. "They're sort of luck of the draw. Everyone who's applying has a chance of getting in—it's how the school chooses to accept and reject. I don't really care. Michigan is still a really *good* school. I mean, that was also one of my top choices."

It was an especially rough year for Aziz's high school in the way of college ding letters that poured in from several university admissions departments. Many of Aziz's fellow classmates were forced to settle for their second, third, and fourth choice schools. Even the class co-valedictorian got the rub from all three Ivy League schools to which he applied. "Our guidance counselor said it was, like, the worst in twenty *years*," Aziz deadpans. "She doesn't really know what to say. She was really surprised that I got rejected from three, wait-listed at two, and that I got into Michigan. She thought I would at least get into *three*. She told me Yale would be a stretch and Penn a little bit, but she told me the other ones would have been *cake*."

On the upside, the long wait is finally over, and at least Aziz has been accepted *somewhere*. He remains determinedly upbeat about his prospects for an engaging college experience despite the fact that Michigan was not his ideal selection. Besides, the Ann Arbor campus is close enough that Aziz can travel home on long weekends, so his mom can still do his laundry (a definite perk). "I'm looking forward to the whole different atmosphere," he tells me. "Take what you get, you know? Because in the end, whether I go to Michigan or another one of these schools, it's probably not going to make a huge difference in my life."

And of course there's prom to think about, which helps keep everything in perspective. The big dance is only a few days away, but Aziz still doesn't have a date (one of the admitted downsides to not having a steady girlfriend when you go to an all-boys school is having to hustle come coed social events). "I'm not the *only* one," Aziz bashfully contends of his dateless classmates. "The thing is it's not that hard to get a date, but you have to find one that will fit into the group. There's a group of five per table so you don't want to bring someone that nobody knows. And since all these girls go to different all-girls schools, you've got to find three friends who want to hang out together for the night. You can't just pick a random person who doesn't know anyone. It's sort of just whoever comes in the pack. From what I hear it pretty much works out that you can go with one person to the prom and then somehow end up going with somebody *else* two hours later."

Aziz's most promising option is the private Catholic girls school across town, where tartan plaid miniskirts and flirty knee socks abound. "Yeah, I'm going to get my bowling jacket and see what I can do," he sarcastically cracks of his nonstud status in combing the school for a date.

In the end, Aziz attends prom in a tux that he borrows from his dad. He rents a silver satin cummerbund and matching silver vest and his date is from a public high school. "It was fun," Aziz languidly comments of the tame night of not drinking alcoholic beverages, dancing to the occasional Fergie song, and hanging out with friends while poking forks at rubbery banquet food. "I mean, it wasn't, like, that *spectacular* or anything."

In the subsequent weeks building up to high school commencement, Aziz focuses most of his attention dreading but no longer *studying* for his AP exams. "I'm taking *five*," he exhales exhaustedly, anticipating a summer respite from the grind of senior year. "I've spent no time study-ing for them. I'm just about at that point in the year where I don't *care* anymore."

Aziz graduates with honors. He fêtes the milestone with a bundle of graduation gifts including a brand-new navigation system for his Pontiac G-6, DVDs, and cash. His schedule is packed all month long with friends' grad-uation parties. There are no crushed Budweiser cans strewn about the lawns at these catered parties. There are no drained bottles of Goldschläger in the kitchen trash, residual gold flecks clumped at the bottom. There is no sex. No make-out sessions. No loud music. No drugs. No girls ripping off their bikini tops. "We went swimming and kind of, like, hung out," Aziz reports of one gathering. "The other one was a backyard barbecue. You know, parties where the par-ents send out fancy invitations. They're pretty G-rated."

It tends to be the challenging troublemakers that we long to better understand, the confused boys that wrestle our tolerance to the ground. Getting to know Aziz, I real-ize what a shame this is, because we can all learn a great deal from his example: How to be happy despite life's set-backs (not getting into your first choice college), how to be content with who you are and not try to be anybody you're not (not drinking, not doing drugs), how to make friends (keeping an open mind).

Aside from dabbling in a sport Aziz calls "dorky" and committing to an informal pro-life posse whose members sit cross-legged on desks in a classroom watching infor-mational videos, Aziz is a polite, smart, amiable kid with-out any of the harrowing, debilitating traces of adolescent angst. These are the qualities that make the "average" teenage boy quite remarkable indeed. Even Aziz reluctantly admits, with a tinge of boyhood embarrassment, "I guess you could call me pretty *happy*."

The
Teenage Dad

> I used to be out a lot on the streets chillin' with my people. I was just in the streets doing everything all negative. I was selling crack, heroin. When she was born I didn't cut it off 100 percent, not all at once. I'm not going to say that I was perfect, but I started to get on track. She got me out of all this stuff I was into. I would be in jail or something if I didn't have a baby. She saved my life.
> — *Tyrone Gomes*

Tyrone Gomes was seventeen years old when he became a father. The southeastern Massachusetts high school junior was seventeen years old when he and sixteen-year-old Lilly began having sex. They'd been having un-protected intercourse for a year. Like a lot of teenagers, they naively assumed that "pulling out" would prevent an unwanted pregnancy before they decided to finally stop chancing it and go on the pill.

"As soon as she got the birth control pill we did the test because she had missed her period," Tyrone recalls, tugging on the lid of his red and blue Red Sox baseball hat. A hand-some teen with African, Native American, and Portuguese ancestry, Tyrone momentarily reflects on the past two years of his life, his almond-shaped eyes peering downward. "After that she was going to start using it," he flatly continues, shrugging off the irony. "But by then it was too late."

It's a cold day in November and we're sitting in a strip-mall Starbucks south of Boston, a few miles from where Tyrone was raised, in a Massachusetts city with a rich history in shoe industries that's also the birthplace of two famous World Champion boxers. It's a working-class urban center with pockets of material comfort but mainly a gritty reputation. Tyrone has just completed a morning shift at his new job finishing floors for a local construction company. His earlobes gleam with little diamond studs, a birthday gift from Lilly, and his eyes are soft and tired. Exhausted from work and the daily demands of fatherhood, Tyrone still beams as he flashes a wallet-size photograph of his young daughter, Roxie, dressed up as a butterfly with sparkly wings for Halloween. "Me and my girlfriend do *everything* for her," he boasts.

When they discovered that she was pregnant, Tyrone and Lilly had been dating for three years. They were raised devoutly Pentecostal and Catholic respectively, so abortion was never an option. From that first flush of two pink lines on the home pregnancy test, they knew that they would have the baby. "Our worries were how we were going to *deal* with it," explains Tyrone.

Tyrone's parents weren't exactly thrilled about the situation but they accepted it. In some ways they even expected it, he says, as one of Tyrone's brothers became a father when he was eighteen. Tyrone's mother was about the same age as Tyrone is now when she had him, younger when she had his older brother. As Tyrone sarcastically quips, "They were already broken in so far as teenage pregnancies go, so to speak."

Lilly's family, on the other hand, was furious, and the couple endured months of alienation from her family. "Her parents kicked her out," remembers Tyrone. "Her parents believe in marriage before you have kids. They were disappointed in me. They were angry at her. I didn't get nuthin' compared to what *she* got."

But Roxie's arrival was worth all of the tumult that came before it.

"It's crazy because, you know, I *made* her," Tyrone exclaims of his depth of adoration and admiration for his daughter. "She's *mine*, you know what I mean? And I want to do everything for her. I just want to be there for her for everything. I want to take her everywhere. Show her the world and give her everything I can. Everything I didn't have and more, that's what I want to give her."

But as Tyrone understands, it's difficult to give everything to a child when you're barely out of adolescence, work a full-time job, and attend part-time courses at a local community college to complete an associate's degree in criminal justice. Until he landed his union position laying floors, Tyrone didn't even have health insurance. He is presently saddled with enormous financial responsibilities and paternal pressures in taking care of his daughter and his girlfriend that he was in no way prepared to tackle at an age when many teens focus on what major to declare in college and finding a date for prom.

"You jump into adulthood a little faster than normal," Tyrone notes. "'Cuz you have a kid. Everything that you always wanted to do—all that teenage life—it just kinda goes away. You gotta work and have a *lot* more responsibility."

Being a minority teenage father not married to his child's mother elicits a litany of negative stereotypes such as "absentee dad" and "drug dealer dad." Tyrone knows this. He confronts such stereotypes in people who are surprised that he's actively involved in his child's upbringing when many of the other teenage fathers they know are not. A lot of the teenage dad stereotypes, Tyrone respectfully consents, are stereotypes for a reason. He's witnessed such stereotypes manifested in other teenage fathers and, admittedly, in himself. For a brief time after Roxie was born Tyrone felt desperate and dealt cocaine and heroin to help support his family (we discussed this in greater depth at a later time).

Many of the stereotypes about teenage fathers that Tyrone and I talk about are grounded in fact. According to a research bulletin by the U.S. Office of Juvenile Justice and Delinquency Prevention (OJJDP), "Boys who become fathers are also likely to engage in a constellation of other problem behaviors such as non-criminal misbehavior (status offending), disruptive school behavior and drug use. . . . teen fatherhood has many negative educational, financial, social, health and other developmental consequences for these young men and their children."[1]

And yet in Tyrone's experience, he explains, raised in a mostly black community where several friends and family members become fathers during their teens, the general attitude is that having a baby when you're a teenager "isn't that big of a deal."

Not that Tyrone condones young men and women having children out of wedlock. On the contrary, if he were to advise teenagers on the subject he would unequivocally urge them to use birth control from the moment they start having sex—*if* they decide to have sex—and not commit the same lapse in judgment that he and Lilly did. "Oh yeah, I would tell them *definitely* to wait," he assiduously declares, "because it makes you jump a couple of years, you know what I mean? I would definitely tell people to *wait*."

However, there is a sunnier side to teenage fatherhood beyond its dark repercussions that Tyrone laments most people in America don't get to see. Tyrone may not be the perfect parent, but he is an inspiring example of a teenage father striving to his utmost ability to emerge from his experience an emotionally stabilizing, financially supportive force in his toddler's life, and not dodge his familial responsibilities as do many of the other teenage dads he knows, including several family members.

Because so many teenage fathers are absentee figures in their children's lives, we don't often hear about the young men who are involved and committed. Paternal pressures, fiscal stressors, and the emotional strain of fathering a child when you're not even old enough to legally drink are extremely difficult. But there is one happy result of teenage pregnancy that Tyrone regrets is not mentioned anywhere in national statistics: love.

"It's *nuts* how much I love my kid," he tells me, his voice flushed with a desperate affection of the kind only a mother or father understands.

Overall, Tyrone's story illustrates the existential effects of what is arguably boyhood's most monumental life trajectory—going from being fathered to *becoming* a father.

"I have no regrets, but I would have waited longer," Tyrone wistfully declares of abandoning his own adolescent desires at such an early age. "Basically the childhood kind of mentality and image goes away after you have a kid. You really *can't* be a kid anymore. I would have stayed on campus at college. I would have gone out to parties. I'd be going out, you know, doing what *teenagers* do."

Following a fourteen-year decline in teenage birth rates in the United States (dropping 34 percent between 1991 and 2005), the numbers are once again on the rise. Between 2005 (the year Roxie was born) and 2006, the birth rate jumped 3 percent among fifteen- to nineteen-year-old girls, a considerable increase in a trend health officials and planned parenthood organizations had rallied to reverse.[2] The increase was highest among black teens, whose birth rate rose 5 percent in that year. The rates for Hispanic and white teens were 2 and 3 percent respectively.[3] National surveys have also found that between 2 and 7 percent of male teenagers are fathers, with teens in inner cities and young African American males at greatest risk for becoming teen dads.[4] These statistics may even be higher since information on fathers is often lacking from birth certificates (if the biological father is not in the picture). For this reason many of the studies on teenage parenthood have focused on the mothers because it's easier to accurately assess those numbers and figures.

Growing up, Tyrone had a tenuous relationship with his own father, who was moonlighting as a drug dealer and was absent throughout much of Tyrone's adolescence. "He was out there, livin' the street life," Tyrone says of his father. "Honestly, me and my father never really connected too much. As I got older I started to see that he wasn't teaching me what he should have been as a father. I was kind of seeing a lot of negative street stuff."

Tyrone's mother and father were constantly at each other's throats. (One striking commonality that I discovered among boys who experienced domestic instability was that their ongoing dealings with parental conflict could be even more troubling to them than divorce because their exposure to such familial strife lasted for a longer period of time.) The fighting between Tyrone's parents got so bad that shortly after he was born, his mother took him from Massachusetts to live with relatives in a housing project in the Watts neighborhood in Los Angeles. While the area is known for racial tension, gang violence, and riots that gained national attention in 1965, his mother hoped that she and her son could begin a better life—away from Tyrone's father.

"They sort of had a messed up situation," is how Tyrone describes his parents' mercurial relationship. "They're split but I don't even know if they're divorced. It's kind of a back-and-forth thing. They would split up and then get back together. Like, off and on. I would be there six months and then they'd fix their little issues and I'd be back here. My whole life has been back and forth. It's kind of confusing. It really didn't make sense to me."

When he was living in California, Tyrone would often spend the school week away from Watts, with cousins who lived in a sleepy, middle-class bedroom community north of Los Angeles (*the Brady Bunch* house used in the show's exterior shots is located there), and he would attend that district's elementary school. But he spent most of his childhood braving the sharp shifts in geography with his half-brother, Shane, a child from his father's previous relationship. "Shane was like my right hand. When I was out there in California that's who I was *with*."

But when Shane was gunned down in a gang-related shooting (Tyrone, who was fourteen at the time of the murder, is one of three boys I met with ties to gangs), Tyrone's world came crashing down. The events of that fateful day are forever etched in his mind. He'd moved back to Massachusetts with his mother a few months prior and remembers the late night phone call alerting him of the news. "My sister—she's not my real sister, but I call her my sister—she called me screaming," he recalls with a flicker of anguish in his eyes. "And I couldn't really make it out, but she said, 'He got shot.' And I was like, 'He was probably acting stupid so maybe he got shot in the leg, you know? Maybe he'll learn a lesson, you know what I mean?' That was just to tell myself that he didn't die."

For the protection of his family, Tyrone remains mum on specifics. What he will share is that Shane was shot because he wouldn't surrender his wallet. "My brother was stubborn," he says through a solemn, twisted-up grin. Whoever killed him left him for dead in a deserted alleyway, where he lay slumped over a staircase for two days before police discovered his body. "It was reckless,"

Tyrone remembers of the months following Shane's murder. "It was just crazy. Everybody was just . . . *sad*."

His brother's death failed to bring Tyrone and his father closer together. If anything, it deepened the rift between them, cementing Tyrone's impression of a man who dragged his family into a crime-riddled world where nobody was safe from anybody and no one knew right from wrong. Where Tyrone grew up, nothing was protected, not even the sanctity of human life. His father, claims Tyrone, didn't seem to care what the repercussions were of his entanglements in crime (at least his mother, he tells me, tried to provide him with a happier childhood by moving to California). Even if his half-brother's death was not directly the fault of his father, Tyrone blamed him for it. He was bereft. When Shane died, Tyrone felt that he had lost everything, including his sense of self.

Many of the boys I interviewed reported tempestuous relationships with their fathers, and having a trusted confidant (be it a brother or a mentor) helped save these teens from self-destruction. In Apollo's case, his Narcotics Anonymous sponsor guided him throughout his healing process; Preston relied on his best friend, and Manuel looked up to his eleventh grade English teacher. But when trusted friends moved away or simply moved on with their lives, the sense of abandonment and disruption was deeply unsettling. Tyrone's father had all but disappeared, and now Shane was dead. And while he understood that his half-brother was not the best role model, Tyrone loved him and valued their friendship beyond almost anything. And now Shane was gone. Tyrone was fourteen years old and wallowing in dangerous emotional territory. He believed that he had nowhere else to turn.

Arnold L. Gilberg, a prominent Beverly Hills psychiatrist, blames part of the inner-city fallout on of the lack of role models in general. "These kids do not have adequate role models or mentors," Gilberg states. "They don't really know anybody other than people who have been in trouble. They have no place to turn. It could be a man or a woman. What they need is a human being. Otherwise, their choices are really limited. They don't know how to find different options. One of the most important lifesaving tools is knowing that there's an *alternative*."

Reflecting on his turbulent adolescence and his bitter relationship with his father, Tyrone believes he has since discovered a sense of peace. "It taught me more than it hurt me," he says of the way his father raised—or did *not* raise—him. "I learned from my parents' mistakes. I try to be different than what my father was."

But a desire to be different, though powerful motivation, may not be enough when you've been positioned as a pawn in a marriage and been exposed to illicit behavior that remains embedded in your consciousness throughout adolescence and into adulthood as an example of how to behave. No doubt, much of what Tyrone endured as a child in the way of street violence ultimately contributed to his own descent into drug dealing, a downslide he's now working to reverse for the sake of providing a positive fatherhood experience that his own father did not.

There's a lot of temptation everywhere, but for Tyrone, being a good father often means averting illegal—and *easy*—opportunities to make cold hard cash.

"There's money out there that you can make," Tyrone remarks of the street hustling lifestyle—drug trafficking, theft—through which friends and family have amassed money, fancy cars, and sprawling mansions with four-car garages. Several of Tyrone's family members in California and Massachusetts have logged jail time for committing crimes. "I could make what I make in a week in one *day*," sighs Tyrone shaking his head. "It's *tough* not to do. I fight that all the time. The temptation. I got a cousin out here and I see all the money he makes and I'm like, 'Damn I need to get on *that*.'"

Tyrone's inner tug-of-war to live his life on the straight and narrow has proven a spiteful battle between what he rationally understands is morally and legally wrong and his father's detrimental influence. "Seeing my father doing that, dealing drugs and stuff," he explains, more as a reference point for his mistakes than as an excuse, "that's kinda what I *knew*."

Tyrone is spare on the fine points of what transpired shortly after Roxie's birth when he was caught dealing cocaine and sentenced to house arrest and a year of probation. "It was just a long story," he dismissively relates, pointing to a small, crescent-shaped cut above his right eye. "I got into a dispute with some kids. They almost jumped me—it was kind of a retaliation type thing. My older cousin that I was hanging out with for a while after Shane was killed and I was back in Massachusetts got caught with a gun and crack cocaine. I got caught with a small amount of drugs."

Tyrone and his cousin both got off relatively easy. His cousin spent a year and a half behind bars for a crime that generally carries a stiffer sentence. "The police would come and check up on me all the time," Tyrone loosely details of his three-month home lockup. "I wasn't even supposed to have visitors but people would come over, keep me company. It was strict, but they let me do a *lot*. At the time they were trying to pin a lot of different charges on me, but then I kind of told the judge, 'I got a kid and she's gotta eat, and the only way she's gonna eat is if I'm *working*.' So I got to go to work."

Tyrone exhibits no detectable anxiety regarding his house arrest, however short-term it was. There's no shame or embarrassment as he tells the story. "It taught me a lot and shows me a lot too. But I don't regret it. I don't know how to explain it—it's just kind of *normal* where I come from."

While his incarceration has deterred Tyrone from committing further crimes and set him on a straighter path, he has not yet extricated himself from the individuals whose influence landed him there in the first place. Tyrone has loosened ties to certain elements of his home community. He doesn't drive around, for example, with people he knows are out looking to score a hit or sell drugs, but he still keeps a foot partially planted inside its periphery. He does not deal drugs anymore, but he hasn't completely cut off contact with friends who do. He feels caught in the middle, a predicament faced by many boys growing up in neighborhoods wracked with crime-related problems.

"It's hard for me," Tyrone acknowledges of distancing himself from the toxic environment in which he was raised, "because when you grow up one way that's kind of what you do. I kind of fight myself a lot to change a lot of things. I'm sure there is a way out, but when you grew up seeing one thing, that's kind of what you move towards."

He pauses for a moment, lightly tapping one of his Air Jordans against the wooden leg of the café table. "I don't think I *can* move away from it," he confesses. "It's not that simple. It's not something I want to do. I don't *want* to jump out of it. It's what I grew up in. It's kind of like a family thing to me."

Boys learn from the examples around them, and while I met many teens exposed to deleterious influences in the way of drugs, street violence, and crime, not all possessed the gumption to deflect its harmful effects as they matured into adults. Boys with at least one parent presenting an upstanding social example fared better when making life choices. Like Manuel (the Optimist), they stayed out of trouble. Those with two morally bankrupt parents seemed to have the hardest time curbing destructive habits. As driven and determined as Tyrone is to change, he still feels the weight of his family history bearing down on his shoulders. He elicits this information not as a pitiable excuse, but as a wake-up call to all parents. Depending on their choices, the debris of a boy's childhood has the potential to derail his chances of creating a domestically and emotionally prosperous life for himself and his family.

"Some kids got a choice," he says. "And some kids don't."

Tyrone hasn't fully fleshed out what he'll tell Roxie if she discovers that at one point her father dealt drugs. Most likely, he figures, he'll simply tell her straight out.

"I'm trying to raise her away from that as much as I can but I think it's going to come up regardless," he posits pragmatically. "Looking at the environment, how it is, I mean, I'm not gonna lie to her. What I'm probably gonna tell her is how it *is* and what *not* to do. I know it's kind of like a weird situation, but I feel like how I grew up, the best advice you can get is to see it rather than hear it. So I'm trying to *show* her the right way by me working an honest job and going to school and trying to better myself. 'Cuz I'm happy where I'm at now. I feel like I experienced a lot and I know the difference between right and wrong. I can't be riding around with my kid when somebody is *shooting* at me."

Tyrone heaves his shoulders forward and yanks on the lid of his baseball hat, a gesture of communion with his dead brother Shane (whose favorite team was the Red Sox) that he makes repeatedly throughout our talks. "I'm trying every day. Because I *want* to be here for her. She needs a father. She needs a role model. My father wasn't here for me and I know how *that* turns out."

One of the most beneficial parenting tools to assist Tyrone in his becoming an exemplary role model for his toddler daughter is a high school program called Project Teen Parents. For the past twenty years, the Massachusetts state-funded program has catered to male and female teen parents working to complete their high school education. Among the group's many services are safe transportation to and from school for the teenage parent and child, day care for the child while the parents are in class, and a bevy of assorted mentoring opportunities such as counseling referrals to various outside agencies.

"It's kind of a support system," describes Tyrone of the program, in which he participated until he graduated. "It was a positive experience."

Robin Thompson, a program facilitator, remembers Tyrone as an "atypical case." "When [Lilly] was pregnant they both came to see me which is unusual," recalls Thompson of their first informational meeting. "Typically I interview the teen moms and the pregnant girls who want to come into the program."

While the program is actively open to boys getting involved, few take advantage. In 2006 there were twenty-five students total, and only four of them boys (a ratio that reflects the aforementioned national averages of teenage fathers involved with their children). For the boys who do choose to participate, it sets up issues of jealousy among the girls whose baby daddies do not take part. "People have to grow up very quickly," Thompson remarks of teenage parenthood, "and some of the guys just aren't *there*. That's devastating to the young women, and that's why it's been such a pleasure to have someone like Tyrone who was very open and stood up, and I think that was a positive thing for some of the other young men at the school to see. He certainly wasn't ashamed or embarrassed. He was proud to take care of his child. And that was *very* admirable."

The program requires each student to spend an allotted amount of time in the on-site day care facility visiting

his or her child (typically during study hall). In this regard, Tyrone surpassed the program's requirements. "He
was there every single day in the day care visiting and playing with his daughter along with Lilly," applauds Thompson of Tyrone's efforts. "He was extremely motivated, and
he clearly loved being with his daughter. Most of the dads
that we have contact with aren't as involved with their
children as Tyrone is. I would have to say that Tyrone is
a little bit exceptional."

Before Thompson headed the program, she'd formed
her own opinions about teenage parents—teenage dads
especially. Take a case profile such as Tyrone's and she
might have assumed the worst. But she soon discovered
that teenage parenthood has the potential to be a vastly
different reality from the dismal wasteland projected in
news reports and on talk shows. Many teenage fathers are
currently setting poor examples for their children, but
there are some, such as Tyrone, who commit to doing the
exhaustive self-evaluation in order to become the best possible father that he can be in spite of his own life circumstances. For example, Tyrone is one of the few teenage
fathers Thompson has worked with who are still in a committed relationship with their baby mama. That Tyrone
wants to promote effective change in his life and has already
taken steps toward that end—including jointly partnering
with Lilly in their parenting duties—are both encouraging
signs, she notes.

"No, it does *not* make him a bad dad," she declares of
Tyrone's prior entanglement with drugs. "Rather, it shows
a maturity and an awareness about what he has gained,
and what he has left behind."

Her work with Project Teen Parents has brought
Thompson to believe that a teenage father can be a *good*
father. Although we all understand the challenges pre-

sented by teenage pregnancy and would prefer our children to wait until adulthood before becoming parents, Thompson is confident that in shifting our attitude about teenage pregnancy from blame and shame to compassion and understanding, we can make better parents out of teenage fathers, with results that will collectively advantage our society. If we can commit to a more sensitive portrayal of teenage fatherhood, then the children will benefit, and this should be a key concern. Education, states Thompson, is the key. "I think having someone like Tyrone shows that if someone does father a child, then the fact that they become involved in that child's life and not view the baby's mother as someone 'who's out to get me,' if they can really see the *joy* of having this life that they helped create and be a part of it," Thompson asserts, "then he can use that energy to make something positive happen in that future. And this is what Tyrone is doing."

Roxie is the spitting image of her father—same sparkling, saucer-shaped eyes, same fleshy mouth, a mop of soft brown hair that springs about in curls. Today, when we meet, the seventeen-month-old is dressed in trendy toddler wear: flared jeans, Converse sneakers, and a fitted denim jacket with floral appliqués on the collar. It's Tyrone's day off from work, and Lilly is at school (she balances shifts at a local drugstore with college courses), and we're at a McDonald's because it's Roxie's favorite restaurant. "Fries, that's *all* she wants," teases Tyrone, gently tugging on Roxie's jacket.

Tyrone arrived late to our interview, joking as he rushed into the restaurant that when you have a baby it can take two hours just to make it out of the house. "It's just crazy," he laughs, lunging into a spirited conversation about diapers and sippy cups and what happens when kids start walking. "Man," he says, slapping his knee, "they get into *everything.*" He uses the words "stubborn" and "smart" and "not fussy" to describe Roxie, and expresses lacerating disdain for other teenage dads who don't assume an active role in raising their children.

"I have friends who have kids and they take it lightly," Tyrone scoffs, shaking his head. "They take it as *nothing*. It's just crazy. I just feel like when you have a kid you have to be there for them. And they're not there for their kids."

He admits that people are visibly surprised when Lilly runs into people and she tells them that she and Tyrone are still together. (She lives with her parents but sees him every day.) "Every time my girl tells people about me they're like, 'Oh he's *still* with you, still with the *kid*?'" People naturally assume that Tyrone has abandoned his girlfriend and child. "But it's not a burden. I just take it day by day. I love my daughter."

This love is evident as Tyrone attempts to leave Roxie with me for a moment to order lunch at the counter. Roxie flaps her arms wildly up and down, squawking a high-pitched, birdlike "Da-da!" Tyrone swivels back around and single-handedly scoops Roxie up and cradles her against his hip. They return a few minutes later with a Happy Meal. Tyrone playfully arranges Roxie's fries on her tray. She flashes a flirtatious toothy grin and then pushes her fries around. "She's showing off a little bit," Tyrone proudly smiles, gently prodding Roxie to eat her fry.

Later he'll take Roxie to the toy store. Sometimes they'll go to the park or to the zoo or the aquarium. "I love wild cats," he tells me, coyly smiling. "They're the top of their chain, they lead everything. It's fun taking Roxie places. I like when she's happy. That makes me happy."

Like a lot of parents, Tyrone loathes the idea of day care, but with Lilly busy with school and her job and Tyrone juggling college and full-time work, it's the only affordable option. Hopefully that won't be the case once Tyrone completes his coursework in criminal justice and lands a position counseling others, drawing on his own troubled youth as a platform from which to teach others. "I'd like to help teenagers," he hopefully announces, "kids in the same kind of situation that I grew up in."

Other plans do include marriage, though not in the immediate future. Lilly's parents are pushing for it, but Tyrone wants them to wait until they've tried living together first. They've recently rented a little apartment in a working-class suburb of Boston, and are moving in together soon. "I'm kind of nervous about it to be honest with you," Tyrone confesses, his voice going hollow in a manner that reveals his vulnerable, youthful side. "It's a big deal, it's a big commitment. I'm kind of scared. She's still eighteen and she can change her mind tomorrow and then what was all the work I put in for? Everyone tells me, 'You got a whole *life* ahead of you.' And it has nothing to do with the love—it's not that. I *know* that I can trust her. But we could be totally different and go two different ways. I just don't want to be a statistic."

But they have a child together, and in that respect are already connected for life. "I'm trying to move closer and closer," he says, fear mounting in his trembling voice, sounding every bit like any other teenage boy not yet ready for a lifetime commitment, "but I'm scared. I don't want to rush into it."

Sometimes, all Tyrone wants to do is escape from the clatter of the community in which he was raised. If he could, he'd take Lilly and Roxie to California, where they'd eke out a peaceful patch somewhere along the beach, buy a little house by the Mexican border. "I just want to go somewhere nice," Tyrone dreamily wishes aloud, in a way which suggests, much more than geography, that such a move could finally rip away the remains of Tyrone's criminal past. For Tyrone, California represents a road trip to a brand-new life.

Roxie shyly bites down on a fry while tugging on her father's sleeve. "It's great," Tyrone issues as a final assessment of fatherhood, tousling Roxie's hair. "Sometimes, it's aggravating. You have to have a lot of patience. But as long as you can be patient everything else is just growth, development, maturity."

If watching Tyrone in this tender moment teaches us anything it's that a more socially accepting and supportive attitude toward teenage fatherhood may be the best approach to helping these teens become better fathers. While fatherhood is not a choice Tyrone believes any teenage boy should make, he notes that if a young person—through whatever messy circumstances—finds himself in the position of getting a girl pregnant and she chooses to have that child, then the choice that boy *should* make is to be a supportive, nurturing father.

Tyrone unwraps Roxie's Happy Meal wind-up toy and sends it buzzing across the table. Roxie emits squeals of bubbly delight. "If she wasn't here I know *I* wouldn't be," Tyrone solemnly states, propping Roxie up in his lap and kissing her on the forehead. "I'd be in jail or something crazy. Maybe I'd be dead. She saved my life. Having a kid is the best thing in the *world*."

The Homeschooler

I probably read more literature while studying at home than I have in any other year at regular school.

—*Henry Platt*

When Henry Platt was five years old, he was homeless, living with his mother and two younger siblings out of a battered hatchback parked alongside the rocky Atlantic coast of a northern New England fishing town.

Homelessness in America is rarely a straightforward story, especially for a kid who ought to be sitting cross-legged on a shag rug in a kindergarten class learning how to tie his Stride Rites and recite his ABCs. But it is a predicament that's becoming all too common in the United States, especially for minors. According to the National Law Center on Homelessness and Poverty (NLCHP), more than 3 million people experience homelessness every year.[1] A 2004 NLCHP report found that children under the age of eighteen represented 39 percent of the homeless population; of that statistic, 42 percent were under the age of five. A 2005 study by the U.S. Conference of Mayors concluded that families with children made up 33 percent of the homeless population in America.[2]

The circumstances that cause an individual or family to lack a permanent address include factors such as drug addiction, unemployment, a health crisis, or a stack of unpaid bills. Falling behind on consecutive mortgage payments can push a family into the street. And recent research from the American Civil Liberties Union found that 25 percent of homeless women surveyed left home because of complications concerning domestic violence.[3]

At the age of twenty-four, Henry's mother was one of these women. A former U.S. Senate page with a privileged middle-class upbringing, Maggie O'Riley married her college sweetheart to qualify for undergraduate financial aid. She got pregnant with Henry and dropped out of school as she and her new husband relocated from the ivy-covered East Coast to the dewy woods of Washington State. For four years, they and their three children (Henry being the eldest) eked out a hand-to-mouth existence while living in a remote log cabin without electricity or running water.

This off-the-grid lifestyle in the Pacific Northwest proved less than idyllic in the end, and Maggie's family members were often defending themselves against the merciless whim of Mother Nature. When her husband's negligence while tending to a wild animal nearly killed their youngest child, Maggie decided she'd had enough. She piled her three children into the car and drove all the way to the Atlantic coast. Henry never saw his biological father again, a man to whom he now refers as "the dude."

At the time, Maggie was estranged from her parents and refused to seek their help. "My mom was in a bad relationship with my grandparents," Henry makes of his mom's determination to do things on her own, extending an empathic admiration for the path that Maggie chose to follow during that confusing period in her young adult life. "Maybe she made a few mistakes along the way when I was little, but, you know, they say the oldest is like the test child. You get a *lot* of experience."

Over the past few years, I have met many boys who were seeking out parallels between their adolescence and their parents' lives, and the connections they discovered presented meaningful opportunities rife with surprising—and often inspiring—revelations of self-discovery. Instead of their parents "teaching" them these life lessons in any strict didactic fashion, the boys I spoke with appreciated being able to draw philosophical conclusions on their own. These boys, like Henry, were able to reflect on the painful choices their parents had to make in a keenly profound manner. Indeed, children intuit a great deal more about their parents than we often realize.

"It was like adolescence," Henry observes of his mom's gutsy decision to ditch a bad marriage and drive cross-country solo with three children under the age of six tucked in the backseat, "but, like, older. She was just wanting to get away."

Too broke to rent an apartment but ineligible for government aid because she lacked a permanent address, Maggie worked the night shift at a local bar and grill while Henry, who was about five at the time, and his two younger siblings slept cocooned in the backseat of the car in the restaurant parking lot. Throughout the night Maggie would duck out during breaks to check on them. They'd shower at truck stops and warm canned meals over a campfire. They managed this way for about a year, until Maggie saved enough money to put a security deposit down on a two-bedroom apartment.

"It felt unclean," Henry recalls of this transient period. Too young at the time to remember everything that happened, Henry notes that it's the hazy, dimly lit details of sights, smells, and sounds that stick with him today. "It was just, like, dirty, you know?" he tells me. "It was grungy and weird. We lived in a tent for a while and I remember a lot of stuff in the tent, having to go get water and stuff, like, down by a river. And then, I remember brushing my teeth by a forest. And my mom working in a restaurant. I remember I'd sit at the restaurant counter. I'd drink a *lot* of Shirley Temples. I don't think I'm traumatized. I think I was just young, and it just seemed, I don't know . . . *standard* or something."

In 2006 Maggie chronicled her family's ordeal in a candid and compelling memoir about how homelessness can hit anyone in America. (Henry remembers that she "was pretty obsessed with being on the computer when she was writing and stuff.") She'd mended relations with her parents, and she and her children were now living in her mother and father's vacated farmhouse in upstate Vermont.

Maggie's confessional became a critical sensation. Suddenly everybody knew that Henry Platt had once been homeless, living in a parked car. Now fifteen years old, he admits that he's never read his mom's book, but the reception it engendered startled him. Like any teenage boy whose mother pens a revealing tell-all in which he's one of the main characters, baring private, intimate details about his childhood, Henry was left with a prickly sense of embarrassment.

"People around town read it and then they were all, like, sorry about it," he recalls, still a touch unnerved. "It was awkward. Because, like, I don't really need any *pity*."

The renovated farm in rural Vermont where Henry and his family now reside is located about an hour and a half outside of Burlington. The White River twists its way around the tiny town. Birds, dogs, foxes, and rabbits bound across the bucolic slice of New England countryside. Tingling, pine-fresh air wafts its way over the hillside where Henry and his younger siblings can often be found herding a flock of bleating sheep, bottle-feeding baby pigs, and changing out the trough in the mud-covered pigpen. During the summer months, they scamper through the grass chasing butterflies. This is a town untouched and uncluttered, the type of wide open space one might picture in a Thornton Wilder play, a place where Henry notes that people "just sort of worry about themselves. They don't really worry about what other people are doing."

A thriving agricultural center, Henry's little hometown boasts its own local butcher and slaughterhouse, where many of the livestock from Henry's farm have been carted off to for slaughter. "It's pretty standard," he pragmatically notes of the pigs and cattle that he's seen come and go over the years. "My little brother cried once, but he got over it pretty quickly because he's so little. It doesn't really upset me because I know that we're just getting it for food. I try to make their lives as pleasurable as I can, but, you know, these animals are gonna *die*."

This isolated, agrarian lifestyle in earthy Vermont— with its steep Birkenstock quotient and pockets of tree-hugging peace activists—is a far cry from sleeping in the backseat of a car. And much has changed.

For starters, Maggie has married a former restaurant manager named Ken. They met while she was working at the oceanside eatery in northern New England. Ken has legally adopted Henry and his siblings, and Maggie and Ken have had three children together.

Ken has become a beneficent influence in Henry's boyhood, coaching his soccer and basketball teams, and helping him with his homework. Their filial bond is not based on biological ties, but a strong emotional connection that springs from mutual respect, love, and tenderness. Theirs is the sort of father-son relationship for whom many of the boys I meet desperately and hopelessly long for. Unfortunately many of them will never get to experience this connection. "I call him 'Dad,'" says Henry of Ken. Indeed, Henry's Vermont-based brood is one of the happiest families I speak with, and he tells me that his relationship with Ken is essential to his happiness.

And yet the monotony of country living, without access to even a movie theater or a shopping mall, can be boring for a teenage boy in his "freshie" year of high school. As Henry expresses it, there's only so much time a teen can spend sniffing the fresh air and running around with the dogs. Sometimes you want *more*.

"Lots of kids drink because there's nothing *else* to do," says Henry, who doesn't drink himself but confirms that the reputation for bored rural kids getting drunk is somewhat deserved. During the long, hot summer months local swains like to get sauced and splash around in swimming holes or go tubing down the White River while working their way through twelve-packs of cheap beer—like a Mark Twain novel with Budweiser. "It's very, *very* boring," Henry reiterates with a tired sigh. "In the summer because there's no school or anything, there's nothing to *do*."

Come September, the area charter school offers few extracurricular activities. With only eighteen students in Henry's freshman class, there are barely enough boys for a baseball team. What's worse, gripes Henry, is that each year the school's student body dwindles in size, with families fleeing to urban centers for more lucrative jobs and educational opportunities. "Nobody wants to live here anymore," Henry deadpans during a particularly disconcerting moment of farm life malaise, "because Vermont is a *dump*."

Many of the boys I met condemned cliques, but most wanted *some* say in choosing friends, and Henry's chief frustration with the rural life is that there are so few kids that it's almost impossible to expand your social circle outside of the small crowd you already know. What if he gets bored with his friends? "Everyone knows *everyone*," he

complains. "You'll go to ninth grade with the same people you go to kindergarten with. There's so few of us so
everyone knows everybody and no one will be *mean* to
anyone. But there aren't enough kids to really have a lot
of friends. You're never meeting anybody new. It's always
the same people. You'll have, like, two good friends from
your class and that will be it."

Henry's first semester ninth grade curriculum includes
geometry, biology, American Studies, and Spanish. He's
neither challenged nor inspired by his courses. "When am
I ever going to speak *Spanish*?" he scoffs. "I mean, I live
in Vermont. Next door to Quebec. There are *way* more
French speakers here. But they don't offer French. I'm
pretty sure they only offer it because Spanish is easier to
learn and to speak."

Henry pegs the school's lackluster curriculum on the
fact that most teachers fresh out of graduate school aren't
gunning to make rural Vermont their educational pulpit.
The school system, he says, has to take whomever it can
get. "We'll get one teacher and then they'll want to keep
that teacher for a long time," says Henry. "I think the logic
is that we don't know when we're going to get a new one.
One teacher has been at school for, like, seventeen years."

On the other hand, Henry notes one considerable upside to a small school with small classes: individualized attention that helps Henry gain a thorough understanding
of each subject. This was a highly desirable alternative for
many of the boys in public high schools, such as Manuel
(the Optimist), who were forced into crowded classrooms
where they often felt invisible. At Henry's school, students are grouped on the basis of strength in a particular
subject rather than by age and grade. "The teachers do a
lot 'cuz they don't have as many kids," Henry concedes
of this educational perk, "and they all accommodate everyone's needs. You just get to know everyone."

Granted, it's great when you're a sixth grader taking classes with seventh and eighth graders because you feel a sense of maturity. But when you're an eighth grader taking classes with sixth and seventh graders, Henry objects, there's little opportunity to advance to a higher level of learning. In eighth grade, Henry consistently felt stymied by the younger students who weren't learning at the same advanced pace, and his middle school experience left him remarkably underwhelmed. He became frustrated and longed for a more rigorous academic environment with more varied course offerings, and that just wasn't being offered to him. "There were times last year in eighth grade," he moans, "when I was just not feeling *challenged.*"

A quarter of the way into his eighth grade year, Henry dropped out of public school to be homeschooled by his parents. With such slim educational opportunities offered in the way of music, theater, and other liberal arts, it's a popular decision, he tells me, among parents and their children living in the area. In fact, Henry and his siblings had been homeschooled by their mom on and off since they were each in first grade. "A lot of people here have been homeschooled sometime in their life," explains Henry of his decision. "I really wanted to leave regular school. I knew I was going to take better classes. I knew it was going to be a *lot* better."

There were boys I met for whom being able to stay home all day and study what they wanted was the ultimate junior and high school fantasy, short of supermodel Gisele Bündchen teaching a sex education class. For some, it seemed like the ideal educational situation: no bullies, no annoying teachers, no required homeroom attendance. They imagined that they could read whatever books they wanted, study whatever subject interested them, sleep well past the ring of their alarm clock.

Maggie, a homeschool advocate, believes unequivocally that it is one of the best ways to educate our young people today. "I don't think school should be this whole stressful thing," she staunchly declares. "Today the schools want you to be good at everything—at calculus, geometry, science. In the real world you need to be good at one thing and do that one thing really well. With Henry I encourage him to stay at home and find out what things he loves to do and do those things well. In the real world it's not about being okay at *lots* of things—it's about being excellent at one or two."

Increasingly, as our faith in the American public school system wanes (a 2006 Harris poll reported that fewer than two out of five adults rated U.S. public schools as either "very good" or "excellent"), homeschooling is becoming a viable alternative for disenchanted parents looking to provide an outstanding education for their children outside of the standard American classroom.[4] The National Center for Education Statistics highlights research noting that in 1978 only 12,500 American children were homeschooled. In 2003, that figure had risen to 1.1 million.[5]

Although only a small percentage of American children are homeschooled, many parents in both urban and nonurban areas are making the switch. As Wendy Mogel argued when we talked about the Mini-Adult, many people are feeling hopeless when it comes to curriculum and their teenage sons. The choice to homeschool teenagers— especially boys—makes sound educational sense to many parents today. These parents ask, Why confine our children to a uniform curriculum crafted by a school administration when we can teach them at home, tailoring the curriculum and encouraging them to learn in a way that best accommodates and complements their individual biological, neurological, and academic impulses?

Some parents opt to implement tightly structured curriculums with set course instruction and rigid homework deadlines. In short, this method takes the classroom out of the school and into the home. But in homeschooling Henry during eighth grade, Maggie deferred to a liberal educational approach termed *unschooling*.[6] "Essentially it is child-directed learning," she explains of the philosophy that places trust and self-motivation at the forefront of the learning process. Evoking aspects of democratic schools such as the Sudbury Valley School in Framingham, Massachusetts, the unschooling movement does not rely on strict curriculums and syllabuses. Rather, it encourages each student to cultivate his or her own niche interests in varying academic and artistic disciplines.

During the typical school day (students who are unschooled do not adhere to a linear 8:00 A.M. to 3:00 P.M. schedule) Henry would spend time playing his guitar and studying ethnomusicology. Henry and his mom would often explore topics in science, while he and Ken, who holds a degree in English and studied Irish literature at a university in Galway, would pore over classical plays and solve advanced-level algebraic and geometric math problems. Sometimes they'd stalk around in nature classifying species of insects or wild birds. While there are state-mandated guidelines for home study (Maggie submitted an end-of-the-year portfolio filled with completed student projects to the state for verification), there are no report cards. Grades aren't the motivation—learning is.

"It's more like I learned *with* my mom," is how Henry describes the difference in public versus home education. "I would do school *with* her instead of her teaching *me*."

Of course, contrary to boys' fantasies, just because you're homeschooled doesn't mean you get to sleep in all day and watch cartoons. "For the first weeks that's what

I did," Henry sheepishly admits with a yawn for added effect. "I'd sleep in until 9:00 or 9:30. But then my siblings were kind of mad that I got to sleep in. So then my mom would wake me up and then I started waking up at, like, *8:00*."

But whatever its benefits, some experts believe that homeschooling (with or without a concrete curriculum) denies children important socialization skills that can only be learned in a classroom, even one in a small school such as Henry's.

Maggie vehemently disagrees: "Socialization is the worst possible reason for advocating sending your kids to school. They can socialize after school with sports or any other after-school activity. They can do that during basketball. I don't want them socializing at school. School is for *learning*." She adds, "My kids are kinder and more respectful when they aren't in school and influenced by just one group of kids, when they are exposed to a wide variety of people and to adults of all *different* ages."

Copious amounts of reading became the core of Henry's eighth grade school year, stacks of books ranging from Shakespeare to Sir Isaac Newton. "I read *so* much," Henry enthusiastically relates, his passion for these classic reads genuine. "I read so many books, usually whatever we could find and whatever we had around the house. I read some of my mom's old college books, and one day we found a biological psychology book. I could pretty much study whatever I wanted. I mean, there was set stuff I had to do, but I could really study whatever, which was *great*."

Whether this form of education engenders in boys an ebullience or excitement, Maggie is hard-pressed to confirm. "I wouldn't use the word 'excited,'" she treads cautiously, "because I find that teenage boys don't show excitement about *anything*. But what I can say is that because he was homeschooled his eighth grade year, Henry is now *way* ahead of the others."

With its crystal-clear rivers and emerald green pastures, rural upstate Vermont is about as far as one can get from the Sturm und Drang of many areas of the country with corporate worries and mile-long backups on congested freeways. But the pastoral pleasures of Vermont's rural landscape are often eclipsed by Henry's itching desire to experience the dizzying pace of urban life, with all of its eclectic offerings in the way of music, film, nightlife, and art. While his family has overcome homelessness, poverty, and estrangement from relatives, and he is grateful for the stable, uncluttered life that his mother and Ken have created for Henry and his siblings (that he has a *home* in which to be homeschooled does not go unappreciated), Henry still feels the occasional sting of small-town dissatisfaction. Rural life can be lonely, Henry tells me, and staying at home all day when you're a teen can add to a sense of being cut off from the rest of the world.

Henry returns to public school for his ninth grade year precisely because he misses its social aspects (as scarce as they are) and the opportunity to hang out with his friends (even if there aren't that many). As empowering and stimulating as self-directed learning is for Henry, fostering strong friendships is also crucially important to him, as it was for all the teenage boys I encountered. Though he misses the intellectual freedom afforded by a homeschool education, Henry is not yet certain if he is willing to sacrifice another year of socializing with friends.

As ninth grade draws to a close and talk emerges of Henry remaining at public school for his sophomore year, Maggie strongly pushes her son to rethink his decision. She hopes that he will instead take advanced undergraduate courses at a local community college, continue with at-home classes, and apply for his GED. "I told him, 'Life is short,'" Maggie recounts following a recent conversation with Henry. "'Why sit in a classroom and have it be all dragged out just so you can talk to your *friends*?'"

But Henry isn't as easily convinced. "I definitely want to go back to school for sophomore year," he tells me. "Even if I learn more being homeschooled, I just don't like being *home* all day."

The
Sheltered One

I am African American. That's what it is in the sense of the word, in terms of my race and ethnicity that's who I am. But I'm different from a typical African American. The stereotype is what you see in American TV, the media, at school. You know, the African American in rap videos, hanging out in hot tubs ... I just don't fit that. It's complicated. I don't share all the ideologies with all the other African Americans at school. And that makes me an outcast.
— *Alain Toussaint*

As we learn from the unflinching testimony of the boys in this book, being popular in high school is no easy feat. Being "ridiculously popular" in a high school of nearly four thousand students when your parents won't let you get your driver's license, carpool you to the junior prom, and won't let you go to movies without them is an accomplishment comparable to scaling Mount Everest. But somehow Alain Toussaint has pulled off the impossible.

While the Mini-Adult struggles to fit in with kids his own age and the Rich Kid wrestles with personal demons while crusading against adult cynicism in the wake of first love, Alain's story presents a unique twist in the adolescent experience. When it comes to his status on the school front, Alain has emerged as one of the most magnetic personalities at his Philadelphia high school while avoiding sycophantic sucking up or tooth-and-claw popularity contests. "I don't know why, but pretty much *everyone* likes me," Alain tells me rather matter-of-factly during an early conversation.

Unlike Alain, several boys told me they felt like social cast-offs, student body riff-raff that nobody would notice if they stopped showing up to homeroom (except perhaps the teachers who ticked off the attendance list). Maxwell, for example, often felt as if his sole purpose at school was to be a scapegoat for other boys' insecurities. Apollo literally skipped school for months before anyone found him out.

Alain is straightforward about his status: He knows a lot of people and a lot of people know him. He is a star player on the school football team. He has close friends he can count on for emotional support. All this, despite the fact that his parents forbid him from going to the local supermarket without them. And while he experiences moments of feeling "different" from the other African American boys at school because of his Caribbean-French heritage (he can trace his family's extended lineage back to Africa, but his main cultural influences come from Haiti and the Dominican Republic, where his parents were born), these fleeting episodes pale in comparison with his over-all sense of being well-liked. Even fellow students and teachers confirm that Alain is the type of kid pretty much everybody can get along with.

Alain's popularity says something on a broader level about boys and race relations, social class distinctions, and how, in Alain's own words, despite parents doing every-thing to protect their kid from potentially detrimental pop cultural influences, he can elicit fellow teens' admiration, curiosity, and an unwavering quest to get to know more about him.

"I don't know why," Alain shrugs when I inquire how he's come to earn schoolwide respect, despite his parents barring him from so much as catching an animated matinee movie with friends. "But I love being popular. It's *great*."

At our first meeting, Alain informs me that his parents will not, under any circumstances, permit him to do any of the following: get his driver's license, obtain an ATM card (even when he turns eighteen he'll have to sneak behind their backs to get one from the bank; if they find out, they'll be sure to snatch it away), get a credit card, go to the mall without them, go to friends' houses after school or on weekends, call friends on the phone for any reasons not having to do with homework, date, ride the bus to or from school, party with teammates following football games, hitch rides with classmates, fraternize with friends at the local Burger King over hamburgers, or walk without parental accompaniment from school to the neighborhood diner down the road where we've scheduled our first interview.

"I can't do *anything* that represents independence," Alain informed me a few days earlier over the phone.

It's the first week of December, and Philadelphia is clinging to the last rays of autumn afternoon light. Right on schedule, Alain's mother drops him off at the diner entranceway, where she will return for him in two hours. She'll phone twice to check up on him to make sure that he hasn't run off with friends or the girl they suspect he's seeing but can't confirm because they've never met her because they *forbid* him from having a girlfriend. Alain's parents both work demanding jobs in the medical field and arrange their shift schedules so that someone is always available to carpool. This tiny window of freedom—two hours without them at a family-friendly eating establishment with frappes and curly fries on the menu—has been hard-fought. From what Alain has told me, I'm amazed that he made it happen.

"I forced it," says Alain, sliding toward the far end of a red vinyl booth. "If there are things that I really want to do, then I have to pick and choose *very* carefully."

Alain is dressed in a gray button-down shirt, charcoal crewneck sweater, and black wool varsity jacket with distressed leather sleeves. His dark, curly hair is close-cropped and shiny. He smiles at me and insists that I order first, then orders a basket of chicken strips and French fries, punctuating his request to the waitress with a polite, "Yes, ma'am."

When his food arrives a few minutes later, Alain pauses for a moment, clasping his hands above his plate as he mouths a whisper-soft prayer of thanks in French, his native language. He translates the prayer into English: "God Almighty, thank-you for the food you have given me. Please, through the goodwill of your son, Jesus Christ, give everyone who doesn't have the ability to eat the food that they need."

Alain considers himself a nondenominational Christian moderately influenced by Christian doctrine in the way of personal ethics. He attends the occasional church service with pals, but mostly for the social aspect. Like many boys today, Alain finds that religion gives him a way to connect with friends; Sunday mass is a time when they can catch up with one another after a busy week at school. But he doesn't need to attend church every week to feel a sense of spirituality.

Christianity does affect Alain's social and political values, most of which he finds are more conservative than the beliefs of the other kids at his school, including the bulk of African American teens. He is against abortion. He's against gay marriage. He doesn't do drugs or drink alcohol save for the occasional wine cooler with dinner. (He views temperance as a "Christian" value.) Alain has never had sex; he's saving that for marriage. However, he doesn't abstain from sexual activity *completely*. "I'm not sexually active in that *sense*," he tells me, hinting at sexual activities (blow jobs) that stop short of intercourse. The boys I talked with were generally forthcoming about their "technical" virginity. Oral sex, most agreed, doesn't count as actual sex.

"I don't even *want* to have sex," says Alain, shrugging off any parental paranoia that he'll head out one night and impregnate some girl. "But that's just me. I mean, if I don't trust you, I'm not going to have sex with you. I guess I'm not like the normal guy. There are STDs, there are unwanted pregnancies, and I'm not down with that. And I have to trust the person first."

All this said, Alain doesn't understand why his parents are so nervous about him doing the things most teens his age get to do. He can't trawl the mall for sports magazines or participate in staff-chaperoned class field trips. Alain's parents forbid him from so much as heading to the local 7-Eleven for a snack without them. While his popularity, he believes, partly emerges from the fact that kids at school are curious to know more about him because he's so scarce on the social front, he'd gladly trade places with them if it meant he could strike out on his own, if even just a little.

"There are inmates in maximum security prisons that have more freedom than I do," says Alain with a light-hearted yet slightly acerbic edge that serves as a coping mechanism throughout our conversations.

Alain has to keep a sense of humor to deal with his parents, he tells me. They forbid him from going to parties, he can't go *anywhere* after school, and when his parents are not at home then Alain and his younger brother are barred from so much as taking a stroll down the street. When his mother works a twenty-four-hour shift at the hospital, Alain and his younger brother are on veritable house arrest. Save for the fenced-in backyard with basketball hoop and a patch of grass, Alain and his brother are on lock-down.

"When they're not at home that's even *worse*," sighs Alain. "You can't even leave the *house*."

Alain often feels trapped with nothing but books, TV, and his brother to keep him company. So far this school year, Alain has blown through an impressive number of classics, including *The Great Gatsby*, *Romeo and Juliet*, Doris Pilkington's *Rabbit-Proof Fence*, and an assortment of romance novels. During a phase when he had an "interest in the ideologies behind racism" (influenced, he reveals, by a racist encounter that he describes in greater detail in a later conversation) he even read *Mein Kampf*.

Sometimes the urge to bust loose overwhelms him.

"Last year," Alain recalls, "it was the summer, one of my friends came over, and he had a bike, you know, and I hadn't ridden a bike for a while, and I was like, '*Ooh.*' Then I rode the bike down the street and came back up. I got in *so* much trouble. I got grounded."

That Alain's family lives in one of Philadelphia's safest middle-class neighborhoods does little to assuage his parents' "over-the-top" concern. Something bad could happen in their absence, they warn. He could fall prey to lascivious outside influences. It wouldn't matter if they lived in an iron-gated compound on an island surrounded by alligators. "My parents are always afraid that something might happen," Alain reiterates. "They tell me I could be hit by a car. Or someone could come up to me and try and sell me drugs. It's the *world*," he stresses. "No matter where I was it would be the same."

Alain says football games "are *really* horrendous." Although an injury junior year has kept the varsity defense tackle on the sidelines, for three years his parents would carpool him back and forth from each game. The handsome, broad-shouldered d-tackle would emerge from his parents' car in full view of fans, classmates, and pom-pom wagging cheerleaders. "I've had my learner's permit for a while," sighs Alain of the arrangement, "but my father now holds onto it so I can't legally drive. I'm eligible to get my license this Saturday, but he won't let me go take the test. I won't be able to drive."

Many parents of the teenage boys I spoke with held similar fears, modern American culture being rife with so many temptations and so many horror stories in the news. On an objective level, Alain can see their side of things. "They're not crazy," he says of his parents, whom he truly believes have his best interests at heart. "I mean, my parents are very nice people. They're *good* people." But he also wishes that their social anxieties weren't at such an extreme level that they monitored his every move.

"It all goes back to independence," Alain explains of his parents' motives. "Making your own judgment without having the experience to do so. They don't like that. If I had a little sister, she would be homeschooled. Trust me. It would be even *more* ridiculous."

Alain's parents enjoyed adolescence with no such social restraints, which Alain finds quite ironic. As teens on the Caribbean island of Hispaniola, Alain's parents were free to come and go as they pleased. Both hailed from upper-middle-class families. Alain's father is from the Dominican Republic and his mother is from Haiti, where Alain's maternal grandfather was a high-ranking member of the Haitian government. They met and romanced as young adults in Port-au-Prince.

"They experienced it," says Alain, a tad envious of his parents' free-spirited youth some forty years ago. "My father, when he was thirteen, he had a nineteen-year-old girlfriend. Time is the essence. There was no AIDS, no worries about sex, and now he takes it out of proportion today by keeping me in the house so I don't get an STD. I've been sheltered from every drug, from condoms. They want me to be straight. To *protect* me."

Many of the boys I met felt they were being brought up with a different set of standards than their parents were raised by. The boys were all aware of these parenting strategies, and even if they disagreed with them, could pinpoint the reasons behind them. Manuel's mother wanted him to go to college because she never had the opportunity. Preston's parents didn't want his college career to be derailed by love the way passionate youth of their generation had been. Even Tyrone was doing everything he could, as difficult as it was for him, to distinguish himself from his father. Like many parents, Alain's were determined to raise him in a way that they believed would guarantee his future happiness. But in the meantime, Alain laments, they were squelching it.

"Parents can be overzealous," notes Raymond Richardson, a Philadelphia area public high school administrator who knows Alain personally. "It happens when some of the parents don't want their own children to make the same mistakes that they did. Many of them do know that life today is more challenging, more difficult and demanding on the kids, and they sometimes exploit their children in the process of trying to protect them. Some of them tend to be so strict that as a result they actually force the kid to rebel even more."

Richardson sees this pattern of behavior commonly in the Haitian and some of the Hispanic immigrant communities in the Philadelphia area school districts where he's worked. With so many schools in America flush with students from different countries, Richardson understands how the tension between cultures can create conflict between Americanized teenage boys and their immigrant parents.

"These parents want the benefits of the United States—the upward mobility, the money, and the middle-class lifestyle," notes Richardson of the tendency for some immigrant parents to be excessively strict, "but what they don't like is that they don't have the same type of parental control and familial control that they had in their home countries where, for the most part, their children would have only gone to school with other children from the same social class. It's the laxity of moral values [here in the United States] that bothers some of these parents."

That his parents are overprotective whereas they benefited from freedom when they were his age but never went down the wrong path boggles Alain's mind. "You had so much freedom and you turned out perfect too," Alain mustered the guts to plead with his father on one isolated occasion. "But it did no good." He speaks good-naturedly, but there's a noticeable patina of weary frustration underneath it all. I've seen it before in boys who just can't seem to break through to their parents, no matter how hard they try. "I don't understand," Alain sighs, "why I have to be that sheltered. Because I'm so sheltered. I'm very, *very* sheltered. I'm *extremely* sheltered."

Alain doesn't own a single pair of jeans. He doesn't like wearing them, he tells me, not even on weekends. This is *his* choice, he confirms; his parents have never told him what he can and can*not* wear (for some reason, shrugs Alain, it's one of the few social freedoms they've granted him). "They wear jeans on days off from work," he says. If he wanted, Alain could go to school in pulverized cutoffs and concert T-shirts, but instead he's partial to a "not too preppy style." This sartorial penchant could be interpreted as one of Alain's only acts of filial rebellion, dressing like a law school student when his parents are fine with sweats, but dressing to impress is actually a rare point on which

Alain agrees with his parents. Reverse psychology in classic application: When the boys I talked with weren't forced to do something, they often did it of their own accord.

"I have to give all the credit to my parents, the way they raised me," Alain asserts. As boys are wont to do, he often shifts his attitude toward his parents depending on the subject. "They didn't tell me *not* to wear this or that but they told me what it *meant*. They dressed properly and I got a sense of how people treat you when you look pulled together in nice clothes and what sort of social response it got, and I made my own choices."

Alain also chooses not to wear sneakers—unless, of course, you count cleats during football practice, running shoes during varsity track, and court shoes for volleyball. He wears the required uniform for the weightlifters club (he currently presses 360 pounds but aims for 400). But he'll never ever wear sneakers casually.

"That's just my style," insists the semiformal teen, for whom comedian Steve Harvey is a style icon. "It's an image. I'm not into labels—as long as it looks *good*. I'm really into suits. I will wear a suit occasionally to school. I love the colors black and gold and red, like, for spirit day the first year I wore a suit. For certain functions I wear a suit."

Cultivating a sense of style is a pursuit that teenage boys take quite seriously in developing a sense of individuality (e.g., Apollo's pride in his $8 Rite Aid sneakers or the Wonder Woman costume Manuel donned for Halloween). From the gang member who coordinates his T-shirt with the color of his Converse high-tops to the Indie Fuck who rejects anything that isn't recycled in a $1 vintage store sales bin, boys possess a desire to perfect an artfully put together look—even if the point is to look like it's not put together.

Alain asserts his independence by dressing more like an adult than even his *parents* do. He shops at men's clothing stores that specialize in business attire and formalwear. He's been known to wear blazers to school and sports coats. On occasion he'll even wear a two-piece suit.

Because Alain's parents forbid him from getting an after-school job lest it interfere with his studies or expose him to people they don't want him socializing with, they pay for all of his clothes, an admitted upside. Alain also gets a $50 weekly allowance for lunch, snacks, and any other incidentals during the school week, so he's figured out a system whereby he can pocket what he doesn't spend on food for such personal effects as a cell phone with a private number that his parents don't know about. Alain views this minor manipulation as justified, he explains, since he's only going behind their backs to do things that most boys his age get to do anyway without having to sneak around, a logic I saw in a few other boys as well who felt stifled by their parents' strict rules. They weren't lashing out, they maintained, just scraping out a small sliver of freedom that made them happy. If it wasn't hurting anybody, they figured, what was so wrong with it?

"I talk to anyone I want," Alain proudly declares, brandishing his secret cell from which he calls his secret girlfriend. They've been together for about a month, but on a limited basis. "I see her at school," says Alain of how they manage to keep a romance going under such impossible circumstances. "I sneak around a *little* bit, you know? I'll sneak off to go her house when my parents think I'm at weightlifters club. Because, otherwise, it's not *fair*."

Alain then shows me his second phone, the one that his parents *do* know about and pay for, and is strictly for family calls. "I only had one phone, but then when I started calling my friends with it my parents took it away," he explains. "They don't want me to have outside contact like that. They like to monitor phone calls. They read everything on the bill. I could be on the phone and they could sit right there and listen to *everything*. So I can't talk to *anyone*. So I secretly got a second phone. Later they gave me back the first phone so that they'd able to keep in close contact with me. So now I've got two."

Eventually Alain's parents discovered his secret cell, disposed of it immediately, and canceled his calling plan. Listening to Alain, poised and articulate and level-headed, it's difficult to imagine what dark, disturbing side effects communicating with friends on the phone might have on him, what terrifying harm might befall him from simple chit-chat with school buddies, but it's not exactly Alain, he tells me, that they fear will make a wrong move.

"They know that *I'm* responsible," clarifies Alain. "They are afraid of everything else. They're afraid of what the *world* can bring in."

When he was fourteen and heading into high school, his parents pushed to send him to private school. But Alain put his foot down. "My mom wanted me to go to private Catholic school," says Alain, "but I didn't want that. I mean, it's not necessary; it's not necessary at *all*. I already saw where my life was going, I already saw how sheltered I would be. I didn't want to be sheltered at school also. You know, with public school, you have a lot more freedom and diversity, so I would always rebel against private school."

So they sent him, instead, to a public school in a neighboring suburb that boasted a stronger academic reputation than the one in his own district, a Philadelphia high school that had a reputation for student-provoked violence and substandard test scores. Alain spent just six months at the suburban public school.

"I left during the middle of my freshman year," Alain recalls, "and it was because of the racism that I was telling you before that got me interested in the idea that people can judge one another based on the color of their skin."

At lunch, the suburban school's cafeteria tables were segregated by race, class, and color. Alain claims that the cafeteria manager would appoint one of its staff to follow the black kids around to make sure they didn't steal anything. "I'm positive," he maintains. At one point Alain even approached the assistant principal with his concern. "She said, 'Are you paranoid?' And I looked at her like 'Are you serious?' They didn't believe me when I told them."

So to prove it, Alain showed the assistant principal everything on his lunch tray—chips, a brownie, milk—and the receipt. He then took the brownie, hid it under his plate as though he were trying to hide it, and started walking. One of the cafeteria ladies chased after him. "Where's the brownie?" she demanded.

After that, Alain's parents gave him permission to transfer to a different school. "My mom was like, 'Okay, *now* you can leave.'"

Alain isn't sure why he has become so popular at his current Philadelphia high school. Freshman year (he entered spring semester after students had already formed friendships) he slid by virtually unnoticed. He was attentive and well behaved in class, but not exceptionally vocal. He didn't have much in common with other African American kids because he didn't wear clunky gold jewelry, didn't listen to hip-hop, and dressed more formally than they did. He spoke French and English where most of the black kids at his school didn't know a second language, often communicating in a parlance of broken street slang that Alain could not fully decipher. They wore sports team starter jerseys and basketball high-tops and there was Alain in a jacket, button-down, and tie. To others, he presented a stark contrast, more the stuffy boarding school student than the inner-city high school kid. He was never shunned per se, but he felt like an outcast by virtue of looking and acting different. Like a lot of boys, he didn't see how he could ever fit in. So it was to his own surprise that from the start, he fared as well as he did socially.

"When I first came to this school," recalls Alain, "I was just, um, a very polite kid to the teachers. I was fatter than I am now but I was never made fun of. I didn't attract much attention either way." Academically, he was also pulling down average grades. "I'm not Harvard material," he admits. "Never have been. I have a lackadaisical personality in that sense."

Alain guesses that his attitude toward grades may be one aspect of his personality that other students find so attractive. "I'm smart," concedes Alain, "but I'm not a threat in the classroom to any of the other students. I will pick and choose what subjects I want to concentrate on. This semester I chose to concentrate all my efforts on English because it's not my primary language, so that reflected on my other grades. I wound up with a 110 average in English and I had 78 in advanced physiology."

But if he's going to get into a good medical school and become a pediatrician, as he's wanted his whole life— despite his parents pushing him to become a cardiologist or gastroenterologist because both specialties command more cash—he's going to need to boost his sagging physiology grade and his first round SAT scores on which he scored a not-so-impressive 500 on each section. "The funny thing is," he tells me, "is that I'm a tutor. I tutor three kids in Algebra II. I don't know why I don't do better in school. Maybe I just don't apply myself."

His parents' view on college is another topic that creates a sense of consternation in Alain. "I'm not going to get the chance to learn how to function on my own in college," he reveals pointedly with a sigh. "They're going to go *with* me."

Come September, Alain's parents will switch jobs and relocate to South Carolina, where they've chosen a small, liberal arts college for him (he's already been accepted, though he secretly hopes to apply to other schools without their knowledge, even if it's doubtful they'd let him go). "It's *their* choice," he says of the school, "not mine."

For teens like Maxwell, Preston, and Aziz, college represents the ultimate exodus from at-home adolescence, a bastion of educational opportunity in which to cultivate their skills and interests, a place where they can take advantage of a campus's myriad academic and social networking resources, sampling sports teams and special interest groups to which they lacked access in high school. But Alain will not likely have that opportunity. In college, as in high school, he will continue to be insulated from any potentially "polluting" social stimuli.

"There won't be anything extracurricular in college to do," Alain informs me. "My parents are *horrified* of dorms."

Per his parents' order, Alain will live at home until he completes both his undergraduate and medical school degrees. "To my parents, you're not an adult until you get a degree," he explains. "So that means that I will be living at home until I'm twenty-seven years old."

His friends, he asserts, don't give him a rough time about any of it. If anything his inaccessibility only makes Alain even more of a hot high school commodity. He's been invited to prom every year. Junior year his parents gave in to his attending, although they drove him. He's got no shortage of friends who regularly accommodate Alain's restricted social schedule to find time to spend with him, but his best friend Jaelen is the only friend who's ever been to Alain's house. Jaelen's parents, unlike Alain's, let him go and do pretty much whatever he wants. "It's a ridiculous amount of freedom," says Alain of Jaelen's loose-strings lifestyle. "It's not that they don't care if he doesn't come home at night. It's that he's *able* to do it if he wants."

But it's Alain, confirms Jaelen, whom everybody in school wants to get to know. Probably—at least in part, he surmises—because they'll never get to really know him other than what they see of him at school.

Alain is so popular that even the gang leaders—who could have easily mocked him for his preppy style—have tried to recruit him. Due to his parents' heritage, Latin gangs have rallied hard for Alain to join. The gangs have gone international, with splinter groups in almost every major city.

"But I don't do *any* of that," balks Alain of the gangster lifestyle. "It's a waste of time. Because once someone in the gang is in trouble you have to be included. I've never *once* been in a fight."

However, asserts Alain, the associations that people make about black teens and gang life, at least at his high school—where roughly 2,800 out of its estimated 4,000 students identify themselves as black or Latino/Hispanic—are not necessarily accurate and, posits Alain, are harmful to the self-esteem of many of these black teens.

Even gang members go to class and some get straight A's, Alain points out, something many people don't realize. "It's sort of like the mafia," is how Alain describes the hierarchical infrastructure of gang life at school. "In a way it's like a small army—you have ranks. But what you see isn't always what it *is*."

Alain knows people involved with gangs, and he's certainly not condoning gangs, but when people conjure up images of black, knife-wielding hoodlums with color-coordinated bandanas he insists it's a big problem. These stereotypes make Alain feel uncomfortable, especially since he's had firsthand experience in feeling like an outcast because he didn't look or act the same as many of the other African American kids at school. He's since learned, however, that there's great disparity among black teens in America and at his school. It's a lesson that he says helped him understand not only mainstream African American culture, but himself as a person. You can generalize one way or the other, he asserts, even among the teens in gangs.

"Some people say that African Americans don't care about their future or that they socialize with gang-related people," says Alain. "'It's economics.' Or 'it's what's to be expected.' Because the way most people look at it, they say that the gang members are just trying to hold them back. But among the people who *are* in gangs, they believe that they are getting ahead in their own way."

Part of the gang appeal, Alain presumes, is that membership makes unpopular kids feel wanted. After all, he points out, gang-fostered camaraderie is much like the friendships formed within other groups, so a lot of kids join for social reasons. Alain knows somebody's mom who started a gang division. In one division, Alain informs me, there are more white kids than black kids, so it's not a race-specific phenomenon. He has one friend in a gang who wants to be a physical therapist. "He's a superior in a gang and he gets honor roll," says Alain of the boy. "I think he wants to go to an Ivy League school. And he's been close to *killing* somebody."

Alain's main point is that not every African American teenage boy is orchestrating drive-by shootings and dealing heroin in the bathroom at school. "Not every African American kid is bumping against some girl in a hot tub. If you're African American and you see those, you know, music videos, you emulate what you see in it. But not everybody does this. African-Americans all over the place are *different*."

Bullies, cautions Alain, not gangs, are the real threat at school. "They have a new wave of bullies," he attests, a disturbing trend that has prompted him to cofound a school group (without his parents' knowledge) that encourages students to interact with one another and discuss hot-button social issues like STDs, drugs, and violence.

"Before it was the in-your-face bullies," Alain says. "Now it's more behind the scene bullies. You don't see it unless they want you to see it. Teachers don't see it, other students won't notice. It will just be directed toward that one person. Like, if I want to make your life a living hell in my school it would be possible."

Alain might not seem a likely candidate to campaign against school bullying. He's popular and confident, and he's never been a victim. But he has encountered many students who have been bullied, teenage boys with horror stories similar to those described in Chapter 3. Because his parents are immigrants, Alain is privy to being a cultural outsider (boys often don't realize how alike they are despite their differences). Alain is sensitive to teens who have been terrorized by bullies because he understands that it's not their fault. It could happen to anybody. His popularity status could slip. One day it could be Alain who's targeted in the hallways.

"I've seen everything," reveals Alain, nodding his head. "Suppose I were a bully. One day I might put glue in your chair so when you get up your pants rip. You could say it was me, right? But then the next day there'll be another kid who puts glue in your hair. And so the funny thing is, nobody ever *really* knows who's doing it."

It seems to Alain that girls are the big "idiots" these days, not the boys. "They are the big menaces!" he exclaims with brio. "The boys are smarter." The boys at his school, Alain says, don't really get into fights anymore precisely because there are guns and knives involved. Except under rare circumstances, fighting on that scale has become almost obsolete. Citing a recent statistic from his high school (girls were suspended fifty times more than boys and got into physical arguments sixty times more than boys did), Alain says, "Girls are the ones that like to fight now in our school."

When it comes to boys versus girls and white versus black and all the other ways people blankly typecast one another, Alain debunks labels and deems them ridiculous. He's black. He's male. He's popular at school. But what does any of it really mean? Alain wasn't even sure how to title this chapter, eventually settling on "The Sheltered One" because it applies to his experience as a male teen and is not culturally limiting. Any number of teens could consider themselves "sheltered" by their parents—regardless of race, creed, or social status. And yes, you can even be *popular*.

"They don't make sense," he scoffs of school cliques and boy-generated stereotypes. "I mean, what are you going to label me as? I'm a big kid. I have a black skin color. Am I African American? Am I Afro-Caribbean? Am I black? You can't define me. I belong to everyone and no one. That's the way I see it. I can get along with everyone, but you can't say 'he's with *them*.' You don't know what to call me?" Alain rhetorically questions. "Well, you should call me by my *name*."

A few days after we meet at the diner, Alain and the four fellow members of his a cappella singing group meet in the parking lot outside a popular Italian restaurant where they periodically perform for customers. The teen quintet performs jazz, doo-wop, Motown, and gospel. The group doesn't have an official name or any set practice times. Its members rehearse whenever they can—before homeroom, during a free period at school, or when Alain skips weightlifting club, as he has done today.

"If we had a proper name and set practice times, then my father would think that meant we were professional," Alain explains of the chorale's low profile, "and he associates professional bands with drugs."

Today, the five high school crooners gather in a crescent-shaped back corner booth warming up their voices. They segue into a melodious rendition of the Boyz II Men ballad, "A Song for Mama," Alain's sonorous bass voice reverberating against the frosty restaurant windows.

Alain's rich, lustrous vocals have been judged professionally strong enough to compete in statewide singing contests. "I made district," says Alain, who also sings in the high school choir. His parents allow choir, but district competitions are too much for them to handle. "It's this competition, you know, where you can get recognized nationwide and then you're supposed to go to New York if you win," Alain sighs. "And I can't go. And you get $3,000 too, for winning. I missed the Washington trip, the Virginia trip, New York, and the Boston one. You're supposed to stay for the weekend in Boston at the Hilton, and I can't go. I've missed district trips six *times*."

It might seem like a shame, he tells me, especially when it would look so impressive on college applications. It might even earn admission to a more competitive university than the smaller one his parents have selected for him. "My parents don't understand that you're also getting accepted to college because of your extracurricular stuff," he says. "It's because of your grades, that's the way they see it."

While a few of his teachers have tried to talk to his parents, he reveals, none have gotten very far. "It didn't work," Alain reports resignedly, in a tone that suggests anyone who attempts such futile discussion is foolish for doing so. "Let's say you go talk to my parents. They would just listen and shake their heads yes and then they would lash out at me." He sullenly shakes his head. "I don't advise people to talk to my parents."

Alain isn't begging for unbridled freedom from his parents. He's not expecting them to step away completely. Like most boys I spoke with, he just wants something in between. He wants to feel that his parents respect his life choices enough to let him make them.

"I wish they were present and understood that there are certain things as a teenage boy that you *need* to have," Alain would tell his parents if only he could work up the nerve. "I understand when they say they've been through it. But they really haven't because things are different today. *Completely* different times. I mean, they can't say 'I've been through this,' or 'I've seen that.' No, I mean, you've seen things, but not the *same* things. Parents need to pay attention to their children. There are certain things you can't let slide but, in my case, you have to be allowed a little freedom."

Alain pauses for a moment, staring around at each member of his singing group, friends from school whose parents would let them attend districts if they made it: "A *lot* more."

The day after our meeting at the Italian restaurant, however, Alain looks back on his statements and has more to say. "They're not going to tell me to jump off a bridge," he jokes of his parents. "They know better. So I trust them. And I respect them. A *lot*."

Respect toward parents, Alain attests, is a rare thing among male teens. "I wouldn't say that it's a lack of respect but just their ignorance. They don't understand what their parents are doing, what their parents have been through, so they lash out."

He may resent their motives, but Alain feels fortunate to have parents so dedicated and invested in his future happiness. "With my parents, it's not really what they've been through," he says, "but what they have done for me. They stay in every night. They never go out on weekends or at night on dates so they can make sure that everything is okay with me and my younger brother. They've really sacrificed *everything*."

Clearly Alain feels conflicted. On the one hand he wants more freedom from his parents, but on the other hand he relies on them for everything—clothes, food, money. It's a conundrum encountered by many boys lucky enough to have a solid support network at home. Teens like Alain want to assert their independence, but how can they when they are still so dependent?

"I'm not going to go without," says Alain. "Where am I going to go? I do have it good for a lot of kids. Because you have to understand, if I rebel against them, they change their whole outlook and they take everything away."

And so aside from the little minirebellions in the way of sneaking off to sing or getting a second cell phone or meeting his girlfriend for a secret make-out session, he'll never mutiny against them. He's not going to run away from home or disown his parents or strike out on his own. At least not for now. "I want to *seriously* rebel sometimes," Alain sighs, "but I respect them. I mean, it has to stop sometime. It can't go on *forever*."

The Future

Apollo doesn't get into a single college. The rejection letters arrive in flimsy thin envelopes one dismal weekend in April. "I'm working on appeals, which is why I haven't been in touch with you," he finally e-mails me. Eventually, in early June, he fields acceptance letters from two colleges, but neither is a top choice. "I'm excited to transfer, is what I'm excited to do," he tells me, trying to put a shiny spin on any lingering disappointment. In the meantime, he plans a July-August backpacking romp around Europe with some friends: Eurail pass, ten countries, and the freedom to explore new and exciting foreign cultures.

As for any remaining romantic attachments to the music that's permeated his journey from drug addiction to graduating from high school to starting fresh at college, Apollo feels reluctantly compelled to move forward. At times the transition from adolescence (as difficult as it has been, it carries many nostalgic memories) to adulthood is heart wrenching, like having to toss a favorite scratched record because you know it can never be played again.

"Emo, originally, was a bunch of fucking skinny guys in their mid-twenties in San Diego in the early '90s who wore cargo shorts and torn-up Vans and probably drank too much and didn't know what the fuck to do with themselves or what the hell life was," he writes to me one day, reminiscing about a time in his life when he felt unique in the discovery of a certain type of music—and movement— that he felt he could call his own, before Emo became coopted by so many other teens and Apollo's sense of individuality became clouded. Perhaps in Europe he'll find new music to love that teenage boys back home have yet to discover, he hopes.

"Real Emo bands either disbanded or evolved," Apollo continues. "And yet somehow, and seriously, don't ask me how, the label 'Emo' got slapped on to this happy-go-lucky fucking bullshit that seriously makes me want to kill myself. I would sure like to see an Early November fan try listening to Blake Schwarzenbach's raspy earnest yelling for more than thirty seconds without running the other way out of fear and confusion. True Emo is dead. People don't even know what you mean if you say the word anymore. They think of fifteen-year-old faggots with black hair in front of their eyes listening to Finch and Underoath. And since Emo is dead, we've *all* had to move on."

Maxwell, the Mini-Adult, gets that 4.0 GPA he's been fighting for. "High school is time-consuming," he issues as an overarching assessment of his freshman year experience, "but it's not hard. There were a few bumps along the way, but I made it through."

His summer plans include a family vacation in a cottage on a lake and two weeks at sailing camp in Florida. "It's nice to have school over with and not have to get up at 6:00 A.M. when it's dark out for school," Maxwell cheerfully relates, the stress of the school year finally lifted. The summer has provided him the time to emotionally regroup. He's learning every day how to strike a balance between his serious mini-adult side and the capricious perks of being a kid. He's been swimming, playing outdoors and going to movies. "It's been fun," he tells me. "I'm . . . *relaxing.*"

Maxwell's perspective on what's in store for sophomore year has turned uncharacteristically upbeat. His new friends have made him feel increasingly self-confident, and his fear of bullying has been mitigated by the fact that he made it through the rest of freshman year without encountering any threatening incidents. Maxwell's 4.0 GPA has also bolstered his sense of pride and he's looking forward to focusing on classes in tenth grade and welcoming whatever academic and social challenges they present. Come September, he promises, he'll be more than ready to tackle sophomore year: "I hear it's going to be a *lot* easier than freshman year."

Come June, the optimistic Manny is working on a bunch of autobiographical essays about the recent updates in his life. The writing continues to be a motivating force; some of this material will provide the basis for a screenplay he plans to write. He and Laetitia are still happily together, having just returned from a two-week vacation to a little town near Guadalajara where they visited Laetitia's relatives. But recent news of his grandmother's mental deterioration and his sister's boyfriend troubles clouded an otherwise free-spirited summer. "My sister's boyfriend is in jail again," Manny sighs, "and she just found out he had been cheating on her. Yeah, how do you think *that* made me feel?"

Refusing to let these incidences distract him, Manny transfers to a Los Angeles occupational school where he'll accrue credits toward a high school diploma. He describes it as "a bastard high school" and says, "You can pretty much make up all the credits you want." While failing grades have ruled out a traditional cap-and-gown graduation, he's determined to get his equivalency diploma, stay focused on getting into film school, and secure the funds to enroll.

As a way to mark a proposed fresh start, Manny decides to get a "flaming giraffe" tattoo. He says that it reminds him of a Salvador Dali painting, of something artsy and beautiful and nothing at all like the "black hole" adolescence from which he's resolved to escape. The colorful tattoo is an auspicious reminder, he explains, of how far he's come in overcoming the obstacles created by an abusive, alcoholic father and an emotionally turbulent upbringing. The gleaming golden-hued giraffe is a testament to Manny's personal strength in mapping out his destiny. Giraffes are tall and graceful, they walk proudly and hold their heads high. They have the largest heart of any land animal. For Manny, giraffes represent compassion, confidence, and quiet determination. "People say I'll regret it," he reports of the flak he's been catching from friends for the tattoo. "But I'll *never* regret it. I'll never regret the person that I was at that moment who got the tattoo."

Nicholas flunks junior year of high school. He drops out, opting to register for the GED and secure a full-time job. "I'm getting my GED because otherwise I'd have to go back for five years of high school," he explains after a long, unsuccessful day hunting for a job. "I *can't* do the five-year plan of high school. I don't really like too many people in the school."

In preparation for the GED, Nicholas has attended an orientation meeting and has been taking multiple practice tests. "It's just a bunch of problems and stuff," he notes confidently. "I'm pretty sure I'll ace it."

He's still taking his Depakote to treat his behavioral disorders even though he's not convinced that it works. "My mom likes it," he reasons equably.

As for what sort of job he's liable to secure, Nicholas presumes he'll land something in the way of physical labor, but really any paying job will do. "I'm not picky at this point," he humbly admits. "I mean, I'm seventeen years old. I don't think it's going to be easy, but I like a challenge."

It's July and Christopher has just returned from freshman orientation at the University of Nebraska. He IMs me a detailed rundown of what transpired: the group ice breaker games, first semester course selection, and finding out who his future dorm mate is, a pairing already contributing to a twisted sort of collegiate teenage love triangle.

"My dorm mate-to-be, whom I've dated, just recently met *another* guy I've dated," writes Christopher, "and now they like each other. I gave them my blessing, but my stomach just feels odd from it."

To Christopher, the situation is awkward and horrible. Who wants to room his first year of college with an ex-boyfriend who's now dating *another* ex-boyfriend?

"They're not dating yet," Christopher tells me, trying to spin an upside, "but they might go for it sometime. My mind is all for it, because if they're happy, then I should be too. My heart, on the other hand, is saying to my mind, 'Shut up, bitch.'"

I assure Christopher that he'll meet someone new, someone better, knowing full well, of course, how trite my advice is. Still, it seems the proper thing to say.

"I know it's true," he replies. "I'm not really distraught or anything. It's just weird. It's scary too: love, rejection, relationships, and just not knowing what's going to happen in the future."

I ask Christopher what scares him most.

"What scares me the most? The whole thing," he answers, "but mostly how I know so little about the whole thing. It's like going down a pitch-black waterslide, where you have no traction and have no idea where you're going. Not only that, but the slide's really too narrow and it's almost suffocating, so it just sucks. I'm hoping I come out into a nice, deep pool of cool water." Here Christopher inserts a *SIGH.* "There's also a chance I *won't*, though."

Preston sits poolside under a rooftop cabana at the posh Peninsula Hotel in Beverly Hills. He's in town with his family for a black-tie dinner honoring an Oscar-winning actor who's a close friend of his parents. Unfortunately, Preston is missing Willow's high school graduation to be here. "We love each other to *death*," he reiterates, squinting hard into the white California sun.

Preston, nursing a summer cold, is already on a first-name basis with the cabana boy, who keeps Preston in a steady supply of his favorite carbonated soft drink. His hair is a bushy mound of sun-fried waves. He wears flip-flops, a slashed white T-shirt, khaki shorts, and a fake shark tooth necklace that's "in the Johnny Depp style." A bottle of Xanax is on the table alongside a copy of Bruce Lee's *Wisdom for Daily Living.*

"I had one night here in L.A. where my anxiety was through the roof," Preston explains, "but I got through it."

When the anxiety attack hit, Preston's heart thumping hard as he stirred in his hotel room, Hart was the one he called. He remains a close confidant and best friend, selflessly making himself available to Preston every chance he can. While Hart has since left New York to attend graduate school out of state, he and Preston speak regularly on the phone and exchange emails. "We should see each other more," laments Preston, "but our lives prevent it."

Preston is grateful for Hart's help in dealing with OCD-related anxiety attacks, but these episodes are becoming rare. A combination of medication, weekly therapy sessions, and an understanding of his illness have succeeded in stabilizing Preston's condition. Most days, he brightly announces, he feels a sense of contentment, of calm. "As much as I hate my OCD," Preston tells me, "90 percent of the time right now, I wake up and I feel *happy*."

Also contributing to Preston's happiness these days is the fact that when it comes to his blooming relationship with Willow, his father has finally come around. "We've decided that I will do most of the traveling," he brightly reports of how he and Willow will manage their long-distance love affair once college begins in the fall. "My dad just told me, 'You can use *all* the miles you want.'"

What Aziz is looking forward to most about his family's summer trip to Syria is the break he's getting from home-work. "I've done *enough* studying this year," he tells me packing for his upcoming vacation, the last before he heads off to college.

"There are a *lot* of people to see," he notes of the trip itinerary. "Everyone has got a million places to go and a million people to see—my grandmother, aunts and uncles, old friends from when I was younger. We'll be swimming and going out at night. I'm pretty excited. It's going to be pretty cool."

He's also excited about college, feeling confident that as a Muslim boy in a Catholic high school he's already ac-quired the social skills to successfully blend in among stu-dents of different backgrounds and cultures. The University of Michigan enrolls a broad demographic of young adults from around the world, and Aziz hopes to branch out and meet as many of them as he can. He's open to exploring new extracurricular activities and taking part in campus social events. But no, he will *not* be partaking in frater-nity keg parties. He's not the least bit worried that ab-staining will hinder his ability to mix with people; in fact, he's confident that with such a varied student body, he's likely to meet teens who share similar ideals. His ethnic background and religious adherence do not change the fact that Aziz is your average, all-American teen, and he believes that he can get along with anyone.

But for now, with two months to go before freshman orientation, Aziz is relishing some free time without the stress of coursework or grades. "There's no worries," is what Aziz loves most about his summer travels to Syria. "Nobody asks anything of you for two weeks. Over here I have stuff to do all the time. It's going to be great just to get away from *everything*."

Tyrone's daughter Roxie turns two in early summer, an event celebrated with a balloon-festooned birthday party and pastel streamers in every imaginable shade of pink. "*Everything* was pink," beams Tyrone of the bright birthday spectacle, "the cake, the decorations, all the wrapping paper on the presents!"

Tyrone and Lilly are currently living together. They've yet to commit to a wedding date. "It *will* happen," Tyrone promises. "It's just a matter of *when*." In the meantime, they've planned an August trip to California so that Roxie can meet her West Coast family. Tyrone can't wait to show Roxie around. "I just want a change of scenery, to clear my head from everything that has happened," he says. "Everyone keeps dying on me."

Since June, Tyrone has lost three friends to gang-related violence. One of his friends was killed in a drive-by shooting. That the perpetrator is in jail is no salve for Tyrone's emotional pain. "My friend is still gone to me," he declares with biting dismay. "All I can do for the sake of myself and for my family is to just keep trying to stay *alive*."

Henry spends the summer at a six-week academic program called Math Science Upward Bound. During the week he boards in college dorms and pursues coursework that includes geology, American studies, and computer applications. "They structure your whole day," he grumbles over the phone during a weekend back home. "You don't get any free time. It *sucks*."

While he's made new friends in the program and enjoys his computer class, what Henry most looks forward to each weekend is heading back home to the farm to play basketball with his friends. Being away from home in a program where his social activities and classes are tightly structured, he says, has given him a greater appreciation for the simple pleasures of farm life and the freedom that being homeschooled offers. Increasingly, he's considering his mom's advice to not return to school in the fall and instead construct his own schedule consisting of at-home learning and classes at community college.

Alain spends the summer completing a management training program at a casual restaurant while taking night classes at a nearby Philadelphia university. "If I'm going to be spending eleven years in school to become a doctor," he tells me, "then I want to be making money while I'm doing it. I am going to *maximize* my education."

Alain's parents are moving to South Carolina come January and they plan to take Alain with him (they've delayed their originally planned September move for reasons having to do with their careers). Unknown to them, Alain is hatching a scheme not to go. Instead, he's working on saving up enough money to finance his own way through a different college in New England to which he's been admitted. There are times when he feels unequivocally certain about this decision. Other moments, he experiences doubt and reconsiders breaking free from his parents' overbearing reign. It's a big step for Alain, one that he's never before faced, a plan that he never before seriously believed that he could set into action. Defying his parents, though liberating in its construct, is certain to present a host of negative consequences. And that's what frightens Alain the most.

"I *want* to assert my independence," Alain asserts plaintively, "but it's difficult. Because if I turn my back on my family, then I turn my back on everything that my family has that I need and that I *want*."

The boys I spoke with entrusted me with their histories and triumphs, their resolutions and frustrations, and their fears and dreams. They presented issues of loneliness and resilience that they'd confronted at school, among friends, and at home with their parents. They engaged in candid conversations and broke out in hearty laughing fits during good times and bad. These boys are faithful and strong and courageous in their decision to share their private inner selves with the world. They show a childish innocence and a startling sense of worldly wisdom. They've taught me far more than I could ever have taught them.

The way boys perceive themselves is often far different from the way we perceive them, and from the beginning I understood that this disparity was worth examining. In the end, what I discovered is that teenage boys, like the rest of us, are complicated creatures, unabashedly human and flush with unforeseen contradictions.

From the self-professed Indie Fuck to the Mini-Adult, from the Teenage Dad to the Troublemaker, all of these boys share commonalities of which they were previously unaware. While most of these teens declared with dreary dismay that they "didn't fit in" with others their age, the truth is that in their collective sense of not belonging, along with several other linking characteristics, they share a boyhood bond. More multitextured than a statistic, more nuanced than a newspaper headline, these boys, like all of us, are full of unexpected incongruities and colorful idiosyncrasies.

These boys are emotional and expressive, creative and strong-willed. They are intelligent, humorous, unpredictable, and sensitive. These boys are funny, insightful, and clever. They are affectionate and compassionate and courageous in the face of confusing life circumstances. They are lovely and messy, loving and lov*able*. They are ambivalent and yet steadfastly resolute. They hold unswerving convictions and constantly change their minds.

Throughout our interaction, these boys surprised me and worried me and often made me laugh. They impressed me and inspired me. They encouraged me to trudge forward with my research when the information threatened to become unmanageable. They gave me creative ideas for marketing strategies and chapter headings. They were loquacious and curious and enthusiastic. They often made me proud. Most of all, these boys were grateful to be able to talk to someone who was interested in what they had to say.

All boys, I discovered, in their stories and in their lives, have secrets to tell us.

If we listen.

Acknowledgments

To my parents, whose love, ceaseless creative support,
and grand financial favors over the years
made it all possible

To my grandmother, whose inexhaustible optimism and
indefatigable, spunky spirit has always kept me going
and inspires us all

To Danny and Jon, the two funniest, coolest, cutest, and
most compassionate little brothers on the planet

To Fenway and Cookie, the fluffiest muffins in the
history of canine creatures

To A, the hottest shrink in Hollywood, the best friend
a girl could ever pay for

To Willieboy, for the ten years we spent together as I
searched relentlessly for clear water

To Jenoyne Adams, Super Agent, for your steadfast encouragement and enthusiasm

To Colin, wherever you are and whatever you may be
doing, for forwarding my manuscript to Jenoyne

To Lisa Frydman Barr, for my first real job as a journalist rat at the *Jerusalem Post*

To Amanda Moon, for her inspiring, elucidating editorial feedback

To the editors at *LA Weekly*, the first to publish "The Secret Lives of Boys" in its original cover story form

To the following for hooking me up with some of the most fascinating, enlightening, insightfully brilliant adolescent boys to ever roam this earth: Iyad Alnachef, P. J. Cherrin, Lindsay Edgecombe, Michael Levine, Tom Ross, Jerald Saval, Steven Vitale, Willie Wilson, and Ron Wolfson

To the following professionals, artists, and bona fide boy teen experts, for their generous interview time and help as I researched this book: Robert R. Butterworth, James Garbarino, Majy Gibboney, Charles S. Mansueto, Colin Meloy, Wendy Mogel, Demitri Papolos, Ethan Pollack, Robert J. Sampson, Ritch C. Savin-Williams, Laurence Steinberg, Niobe Way, and Lynn Winkler

To all my friends and family who've read every last piece of drivel and were kind enough to compliment what I wrote or at least pretend to like it

To all my old writing teachers who told me that I had talent and that someday I would make it. Thank you.

To all the boys. This book is yours.

And to Paul, with whom I made it out of the narrows, for everything, including the idea for this book

Notes

Introduction

1. Author's definition.

2. David Von Drehle, "The Myth About Boys: Experts Say Boys Are in Trouble. Here's Why They've Got It Wrong," *Time,* July 26, 2007, www.time.com/time/magazine/article/ 0,9171,1647452,00.html (accessed February 16, 2008).

3. Substance Abuse and Mental Health Services Administration, *Results from the 2006 National Survey on Drug Use and Health: National Findings,* NSDUH Series H-32, DHHS Publication no. SMA 07–4293 (Rockville, MD: Office of Applied Studies, 2007), figure 2.5.

4. Niobe Way, telephone interview by author, June 21, 2007.

5. James Garbarino and Claire Bedard, *Parents Under Siege: Why You Are the Solution, Not the Problem in Your Child's Life* (New York: Touchstone/Simon & Schuster, 2002), 97.

6. Garbarino and Bedard, *Parents Under Siege,* 97–105.

The Indie Fuck

1. University of Michigan, Institute for Social Research, "Overall, Illicit Drug Use by American Teens Continues Gradual Decline in 2007," University of Michigan. http://monitoringthe future.org/pressreleases/07drugpr.pdf (accessed September 15, 2008).

2. The National Institute on Drug Abuse (NIDA), U.S. Department of Health and Human Services, NIDA Research Report, *Methamphetamine Abuse and Addiction,* NIH Publication no. 06–4210, September 2006.

3. National Institute of Mental Health (NIMH), *Attention Deficit Hyperactivity Disorder: Introduction,* April 3, 2008, www .nimh.nih.gov/health/publications/adhd/complete-publication .shtml (accessed July 2008).

4. Drug Abuse Warning Network (DAWN), New DAWN Report, *Emergency Department Visits Involving Nonmedical Use*

of Selected Pharmaceuticals 29 (2006): table 1, http://dawninfo
.samhsa.gov/pubs/shortreports/ (accessed July 2006).

5. While open to arranging our meetings for this book,
Apollo's mother opted not to be interviewed.

6. Robert R. Butterworth, telephone interview by author,
Summer 2005.

7. Polysexual means feeling attracted to or sexually aroused by
a variety of different objects, lifestyles, or activities, for example,
learning, reading, gardening, massage, and so on, www.urban
dictionary.com/define.php?term=polysexuality (accessed May 29, 2008).

8. Lev Grossman, "The Secret Love Lives of Teenage Boys,"
Time, August 27, 2006.

9. Ethan Pollack, interview by author, Needham,
Massachusetts, February 27, 2007.

The Mini-Adult

1. Department of Health and Human Services Centers for
Disease Control and Prevention, "Youth Risk Behavior
Surveillance—United States 2005," *Morbidity and Mortality
Weekly Report,* vol. 55, no. SS-5, June 9, 2006, www.cdc.gov/
mmwr/PDF/SS/SS5505.pdf (accessed June 7, 2006).

2. Journal of the American Medical Association, *World Health
Organization's Health Behaviour in School-Aged Children
Survey,* 1998, April 25, 2001.

3. National Education Association, Washington, D.C.
Adapted from prepublication data derived from the 2005–2006
administration of the survey *Status of the American Public School
Teacher* (courtesy of the National Education Association).

4. Thomas S. Dee, "The Why Chromosome," *Education Next:
A Journal of Opinion and Research,* Fall 2006, www.hoover.org/
publications/ednext/3853842.html (accessed June 1, 2008).

5. Wendy Mogel, telephone interview by author, April 29, 2007.

The Optimist

1. National Institute on Alcohol Abuse and Alcoholism,
National Longitudinal Alcohol Epidemiologic Survey (NLAES)
(National Institutes of Health, 2000).

2. U.S. Census Bureau, *U.S. Census Current Population Report
on Custodial Mothers and Fathers and Their Child Support,* 2000, www
.census.gov/main/www/cen2000.html (accessed January 10, 2008).

3. Fathers and Families, Information Resources: Basic Facts, 2008, www.fathersandfamilies.org/site/infores.php (accessed June 1, 2008).

4. Patricia Hersch, *A Tribe Apart: A Journey into the Heart of American Adolescence* (New York: Ballantine, 1998).

The Troublemaker

1. Robert J. Sampson, telephone interview by author, July 2008.

2. National Campaign to Prevent Teen Pregnancy, *Keeping the Faith: The Role of Religion and Faith Communities in Preventing Teen Pregnancy*, 2001.

3. U.S. Department of Health and Human Services, Centers for Disease Control and Prevention, *Summary Health Statistics for U.S. Children: National Health Interview Survey*, 2006, appendix 3, table 6. Vital and Health Statistics, September 2007, www.cdc .gov/nchs/data/series/sr_10/sr10_234.pdf (accessed May 2008).

4. American Academy of Child and Adolescent Psychiatry, *Facts for Families: Children with Oppositional Defiant Disorder* (Washington, D.C.: AACAP, 2008), www.aacap.org/cs/root/ facts_for_families/children_with_oppositional_defiant_disorder (accessed June 2008).

5. Demitri Papolos, M.D., email message to author, July 23, 2007.

6. National Institute of Mental Health, *The Numbers Count: Mental Disorders in America* (Bethesda, MD: National Institute of Mental Health, 2008), www.nimh.nih.gov/health/publications/ the-numbers-count-mental-disorders-in-america.shtml#Bipolar (accessed October 17, 2008).

The Gay, Vegan, Hearing-Impaired Republican

1. R. C. Savin-Williams, *The New Gay Teenager (Adolescent Lives)* (Cambridge: Harvard University Press, 2006).

2. Ritch Savin-Williams, telephone interview by author, April 11, 2007.

3. Alfred C. Kinsey et al., *Sexual Behavior in the Human Male* (Philadelphia: Saunders, 1948), 636–659.

4. Bruce Coville, "Am I Blue?" in *Am I Blue? Coming Out from the Silence,* ed. Marion Dane Bauer (New York: HarperCollins Children's Books, 1994), 1–18.

The Rich Kid

1. *National Mental Association Fact Sheet: Obsessive-Compulsive Disorder,* www1.nmha.org/infoctr/factsheets/33.cfm (accessed February 11, 2008).

2. Judith Rapoport, "About Mental Illness: Obsessive-Compulsive Disorder," www.nami.org/Template.cfm?Section= By_Illness&Template=/TaggedPage/TaggedPageDisplay.cfm&TPL ID=54&ContentID=23035 (accessed June 2, 2008).

3. Charles S. Mansueto, telephone interview by author, June 3, 2008.

4. "Obsessive-Compulsive Disorder," *JAMA,* October 27, 2004, http://jama.ama-assn.org/cgi/content/full/292/16/2040 (accessed June 2, 2008).

5. Trichotillomania (TTM) is an impulse disorder that causes people to pull out the hair from their scalp, eyelashes, eyebrows, or other parts of the body, resulting in noticeable bald patches, www.trich.org/about_trich (accessed June 2, 2008).

6. Body dysmorphic disorder (BDD) is characterized by an excessive preoccupation with a real or imagined defect in your physical appearance, www.mayoclinic.com/health/ body-dysmorphic-disorder/DS00559 (accessed June 1, 2008).

7. Tourette syndrome (TS) is a neurological disorder characterized by repetitive, stereotyped, involuntary movements and vocalizations called tics, www.ninds.nih.gov/disorders /tourette/detail_tourette.htm#106743231 (accessed October, 17, 2008).

8. Glenn Sacks, "Boys or Girls—Pick Your Victim," *Los Angeles Times,* March 20, 2005, www.latimes.com/news/print edition/suncommentary/la-op-boys20mar20,1,3540500.story (accessed June 1, 2008).

9. Majy Gibboney, interview by author, Los Angeles, June 7, 2006.

10. Prozac (fluoxetine hydrochloride) belongs to a class of serotonin reuptake inhibitors (SSRIs) often used in patients with obsessive-compulsive disorder, www.drugdigest.org/DD/DVH/ Uses/0,3915,275%7CFluoxetine,00.html.

Luvox (fluvoxamine) is also an SSRI used to treat obsessive-compulsive disorder, www.medicinenet.com/fluvoxamine/article.htm.

Xanax is an antianxiety medication belonging to a class of benzodiazepines often used to treat anxiety and panic disorders, www.pfizer.com/files/products/uspi_xanax.pdf.

11. Cialis (tadalafil) is a medication used to treat the symptoms of erectile dysfunction (ED), www.cialis.com/index.jsp.

The Teenage Dad

1. Terence P. Thornberry et al., *Teenage Fatherhood and Delinquent Behavior,* Office of Juvenile Justice and Delinquency Prevention, *Youth Development Series,* January 2000, www.nlpoa.org/Office_of_Juvenile_Justice_Program_Washington _DC_Teenage_Fatherhood_and_Delinquent_Behavior_NLPOA .pdf (accessed July 8, 2008).

2. B. D. Hamilton, J. A. Martin, and S. J. Ventura, "Births: Preliminary Data for 2006," *National Vital Statistics Reports* 56, no 7 (2007).

3. Hamilton, Martin, and Ventura, "Births."

4. Thornberry et al., *Teenage Fatherhood.*

The Homeschooler

1. National Law Center on Homelessness and Poverty, *Homelessness and Poverty in America: Overview* (Washington, D.C., 2008), www.nlchp.org/hapia.cfm (accessed July 2, 2008).

2. National Coalition for the Homeless, NCH Fact Sheet no. 3, 2007, www.nationalhomeless.org/publications/facts/Whois.pdf.

3. NCH Fact Sheet 3.

4. Harris Interactive, Inc., *The Harris Poll,* no. 29, April 14, 2006, Table 4, "Evaluation of Quality of Education Provided in the United States," http://www.harrisinteractive.com/harris_poll /index.asp?PID=653 (accessed December 3, 2008).

5. National Center for Education Statistics, U.S. Department of Education Institute of Education Sciences, Washington, D.C., http://nces.ed.gov/search/?output=xml_no_dtd&site=nces&client =nces&q=1%2E1++million+children+homeschooled+2003 (accessed December 3, 2008).

6. "What Is Unschooling?" www.unschooling.com (accessed February 13, 2008).

Index